Character-Based Writing Lessons In Structure & Style

Daniel K. Weber

Avavoss

First Edition © March 2007
Institute for Excellence in Writing, Inc.

Copyright © 2007 Daniel K. Weber
ISBN-10: 0-9779860-4-7
ISBN-13: 978-0-9779860-4-0

The purchase of this book entitles its owner to one free downloadable copy of *The Student Resource Notebook.*
Go to: www.excellenceinwriting.com/SRN

Our Duplicating/Copying Policy:

All rights reserved.

No part of this book may be reproduced, stored in a retrieval system, or transmitted in any form or by any means, electronic, mechanical, photocopying, recording, or otherwise, without the prior written permission of the author, except as provided by USA copyright law and the specific policy below:

Home use: You may freely copy our materials for use by multiple children within your immediate family, or purchase additional books so all children have one of their own.
Small group or co-op classes: Each participating student or family is required to purchase a book.
Classroom teachers: Each teacher and student is required to have his or her own book.
Library use: Printed materials may be checked out of a lending library provided patrons agree not to make copies.

Institute for Excellence in Writing
8799 N. 387 Road
Locust Grove, OK 74352
800.856.5815
www.excellenceinwriting.com

Accessing Your Download

The purchase of this book entitles its owner to one free downloadable copy of the *Student Resource Notebook*. To download your complimentary e-book, please follow the directions below:

1. Go to our website, www.excellenceinwriting.com
2. Log in to your online customer account. If you do not have an account, you will need to create one.
3. After you are logged in, go to this web page: www.excellenceinwriting.com/SRN
4. Click on the red download arrow.
5. You will be taken to your File Downloads page. Click on the file name and the e-book will download onto your computer.

Please note: You are free to download and print this *Student Resource Notebook* file as many times as needed for use within *your immediate family*. However, this information is proprietary and we are trusting you to be on your honor to not share it with anyone. Each family is required to purchase their own set of student materials. Thank you.

If you have any difficulty receiving this download after going through the steps above, please call (800) 856-5815.

Institute for Excellence in Writing, LLC
8799 N. 387 Road
Locust Grove, OK 74352

Contents

Introduction...5
Unit I: Note Taking..9
    Lesson 1: The Story of Mother Teresa Begins
    Lesson 2: Mother Teresa Makes a Difference
Unit II: Writing From Notes..15
    Lesson 3: President Lincoln's Favorite Poem
    Lesson 4: The Simplicity and Humility of St. Francis
    Lesson 5: Abraham's Proclamations During the Civil War
Unit III: Summarizing Narrative Stories...29
    Lesson 6: Mother Teresa Speaks on Abortion
    Lesson 7: Abraham and the Town Bully
    Lesson 8: St. Francis and the Animals
    Lesson 9: Mother's Shoes are Hard to Fill
Unit IV: Summarizing References...51
    Lesson 10: Abraham Speaks on Temperance
    Lesson 11: The Faith of St. Francis
Stylistic Decorations..65
Unit V: Writing Stories From Pictures..69
    Lesson 12: The Sixteenth President of the United States
    Lesson 13: Mother Teresa in the Streets of Calcutta
    Lesson 14: The Character of St. Francis
Unit VI: Research Reports..85
    Lesson 15: Abraham and Austin Gollaher
    Lesson 16: Mother Teresa Receives for the Poor
    Lesson 17: Francis and the Wolf
Unit VII: Creative Writing...97
    Lesson 18: The Civil War
    Lesson 19: A Warning of the Assassination to Come
    Lesson 20: The Key Virtues of a Strong Character
Unit VIII: Essay Composition..109
    Lesson 21: The Faith of St. Francis Completed
    Lesson 22: What are the Responsibilities of a Christian?
Critique Vocabulary Thesaurus...115
Unit IX: Writing Reviews/Critiques..119
    Lesson 23: Mother Teresa Revisited
    Lesson 24: The Gettysburg Address
Helpful Lists
    Key Virtues   (pg. 12)
    "Banned" Words   (pgs. 26 & 38)
    Preposition List   (pg. 48)
    Adverb List   (pgs. 103 & 104)

Acknowledgements

My dear friend, Andrew Pudewa, provided support and guidance during the creation of this book. It is his foundational program for teaching writing upon which the lessons of this book are structured. I am grateful for Andrew's loving kindness, enthusiasm, vision, creativity, wisdom, and devotion.

I also want to thank Julia Pudewa for her artistic contribution to Unit V: Writing Stories from Pictures. Those wonderful sketches are the product of her gifted hand.

To the Student...

These lessons are designed to help you strengthen your composition skills using readings from selections associated with the lives of Mother Teresa, Abraham Lincoln and St. Francis. I have tried to select stories, excerpts, and historical references that are both interesting and important. I hope you will enjoy the lessons that follow.

Almost every lesson has source text for you to read before you start your assignments. After you have read the source text for a given lesson, please do the assignments in the order they appear. Each lesson builds upon the previous ones, as the checksheets clearly show. The checksheets are meant as guides – use them to remind yourself of the skills you have already learned and to make sure you have incorporated new skills into your compositions.

Spaces for your outlines are provided throughout, however, it may be more convenient to use a separate sheet of paper. This will eliminate the hassle of flipping back and forth from the source text to your outline as you work along.

Some of the later lessons will seem to skip a step in the assignment section. For instance, the assignment may simply say to write a composition. However, by that time, you should already know the model and the process: you must still make a note outline, write at least two drafts, and keep your final composition in the back of this book, or in a special folder.

If something isn't clear, don't hesitate to ask your parent or teacher for help. Discuss each lesson with them. This is not meant to be a workbook that you use all by yourself; it is a book of lessons that should be used under the guidance of your parent or teacher.

Above all, have fun. Say a prayer before you begin each lesson, asking the Lord to direct and inspire you as you read and write. Do your work for the glory of God, and you will be blessed. Peace in Christ.

To the Parent and Teacher...

This book is intended primarily for use with IEW's Teaching Writing: Structure and Style program. If you are not familiar with that course, you may find this book difficult to use. Along those lines, it is important to understand that this is not a workbook that will teach the student writing. It is a collection of lessons that you, the teacher, can use to teach writing. You are the critical element for success with this book.

You will notice that I have included a variety of source text material on three carefully selected historical figures. These three individuals exemplify particular character traits that we would all like to emulate and make our own. Reading about these traits and then writing about these traits has the power to assist young minds in the formation and personalization of these traits.

Different students require different levels of challenge. This book provides checksheets at three levels: Level A – beginner, Level B – intermediate, and Level C – advanced. Level A students progress through the lessons focusing on the fundamentals of style. Level B students are expected to learn the fundamentals and build upon these skills with more detail. Level C students should already be familiar with (or quickly learn) the basics of the skills taught, have a firm grasp of grammar, and be able to employ the advanced techniques which are taught in this book. The checksheets for each lesson, however, are suggested. If your students work at a different pace, that's okay. The lessons aren't rigid. You should adjust the checksheet to include or exclude skills as you progress. The flexibility makes this an ideal book for teaching mixed grade groups.

Some of the punctuation or grammar taught in this book may differ slightly from what you have learned before or normally practice in your home or classroom. You are the teacher, and it is your prerogative to teach your students what you want them to learn. If, for example, you disagree with the absence of a comma before a particular "who/which" clause, put it in. If you believe firmly in using "because" instead of "since" (or vice versa), teach it. These lessons are not meant to be authoritative about grammar and usage, but to be a source of ideas, models, and techniques to broaden composition experience and aptitude.

As you may have noticed, the checksheets throughout the book do not have a section to assign grades. The model checksheet on the next page includes a grading system for those who wish to grade their students' compositions.

Above all, be joyful. Smile and laugh as you teach. Teach with prayer and patience, joy and love.

(Model) Graded Checksheet for Lesson 3

Levels A, B, & C **Presentation** ___ title centered and underlined (2) ___ name, date (1) ___ clearly presented (1) **Mechanics** ___ indent paragraphs (1) ___ complete sentences (2) ___ capitals (uppercase) (2) ___ punctuation (2) **Style Tools** ___ underline dress-ups (one of each) (1)	**Level A** **Dress-Ups** "-ly" word ___ (2) "who/which" clause ___ (2) **Level B** **Dress-Ups** "-ly" word ___ (2) "who/which" clause ___ (2) no "to be" verbs with "who/which" clause ___ (2) **Level C** **Dress-Ups** "-ly" word ___ (2) "who/which" clause ___ (2) invisible "who/which" clause ___ (2) no "to be" verbs with "who/which" clause ___ (2)

	Style Point Totals	Total Points	Your Grade
Level A	___/4	___/16	A = 90% - 100% B = 80% - 90% C = 70% - 80% D = 60% - 70% F = 0% - 60%
Level B	___/6	___/18	
Level C	___/8	___/20	

If you wish to grade your students' writing, you may assign points to each of the items on the checksheet. To obtain grade percentages: divide the total number of points the student earns by the number of points possible. Then multiply by 100 to get the percentage. For example, if a Level B student received 5 style points and 15 points total, the percentage would be 83.33%, a B.

Unit I: Note Taking
Lesson 1: The Story of Mother Teresa Begins

Objective
To learn how to take notes in an outline format, using Roman numerals and Arabic numbers.

Source Text

> Mother Teresa was born Agnes Gonxha Bojaxhiu in Skopje, Macedonia, on August 27, 1910. Her family was of Albanian descent. At the age of twelve, she felt strongly the call of God. She knew she had to be a missionary to spread the love of Christ. At the age of eighteen she left her parental home in Skopje and joined the Sisters of Loreto, an Irish community of nuns with missions in India. After a few months' training in Dublin she was sent to India, where on May 24, 1931, she took her initial vows as a nun.
>
> From 1931 to 1948 Mother Teresa taught at St. Mary's High School in Calcutta. But the suffering and poverty she glimpsed outside the convent walls made a deep impression on her. In 1948 she received permission from her superiors to leave the convent school and devote herself to working among the poorest of the poor in the slums of Calcutta. Although she had no funds, she depended on Divine Providence, and started an open-air school for slum children. Soon voluntary helpers joined her, and financial support was also forthcoming. This made it possible for her to extend the scope of her work.

Assignment
1. Read the source text.
2. Reread.
3. Circle the words that appear in the note outline below. The words that you circle are called key words. These words convey meaning in a sentence. When you create your outlines, choose key words to help you remember the main ideas of the sentence or verses on which you are taking notes.

Structural Tools and Suggestions
Use Roman numerals (I, II, etc.) for each new paragraph and Arabic numbers (1, 2, 3) for details. Use no more than five details per paragraph, with one to three key words per detail, or note.

Note Outline Model: The Story of Mother Teresa Begins
    I. *Mother Teresa, Macedonia, 8/27/1910*
        1. *Albanian descent*
        2. *12, God called*
        3. *missionary, spread, ♥Christ*

        4. *18, Sisters of Loreto, Irish, nun*
        5. *Dublin ⇨ India, vows*

  II. *Taught high school*
        1. *Poverty, impression*
        2. *Left school, devote poor*
        3. *Providence, slum school*
        4. *Volunteers, donations*
        5. *Possible, extend scope*

Lesson 2: Mother Teresa Makes a Difference

Objective
To learn to take notes while limiting yourself to main ideas.

Source Text

On October 7, 1950, Mother Teresa received permission to start her own order, "The Missionaries of Charity", whose primary task was to love and care for those persons nobody was prepared to look after. In 1965 the Society became an International Religious Family by a decree of Pope Paul VI. Today the order comprises Active and Contemplative branches of Sisters and Brothers in many countries. In 1963 both the Contemplative branch of the Sisters and the Active branch of the Brothers were founded. In 1979 the Contemplative branch of the Brothers was added, and in 1984 the Priest branch was established.

The Society of Missionaries has spread all over the world, including the former Soviet Union and Eastern European countries. They provide effective help to the poorest of the poor in a number of countries in Asia, Africa, and Latin America. They undertake relief work in the wake of natural catastrophes such as floods, epidemics, and famine, and for refugees. The order also has houses in North America, Europe and Australia, where they take care of the shut-ins, alcoholics, homeless, and AIDS sufferers. The Missionaries of Charity throughout the world are aided and assisted by Co-Workers who became an official International Association on March 29, 1969. By the 1990s there were over one million Co-Workers in more than 40 countries. Along with the Co-Workers, the lay Missionaries of Charity try to follow Mother Teresa's spirit and charism in their families.

Mother Teresa's work has been recognized and acclaimed throughout the world, and she has received a number of awards and distinctions, including the Pope John XXIII Peace Prize (1971) and the Nehru Prize for her promotion of international peace and understanding (1972). She also received the Balzan Prize (1979) and the Templeton and Magsaysay awards. She won the Nobel Peace Prize in 1979.

Assignment
1. Read the source text and study the note outline model for paragraph number one.
2. Circle the words that appear in paragraph number one and in the note outline model. Circle the words or abbreviations in the note outline that do not appear in the text. These words are paraphrased or abbreviated from the text, which means they convey the same meaning in different (and fewer) words. For example, in lesson #1 the source text, second to last line read, "financial support was also forthcoming". We used the word "donations" in our first note outline model to convey the same meaning.
3. Make a key word outline for the second paragraph, using the same idea of limiting each detail to no more than three words.
4. Verbally tell back this portion of the story to your teacher or parent by looking at your key word outline and making the notes into complete sentences. Add in as much detail as you can, but don't worry about remembering all the details. If you need to stop and read the original source text again, that's fine.

Note Outline Model 2

I. 1950, Mother Teresa, The Missionaries of Charity
   1. love, care, unwanted
   2. 1965, IRF, Pope Paul VI
   3. Active, Contemplative, everywhere
   4. 1963, Cont. Sr., Active Bro.
   5. 1979, Cont. Bro., 1984 – Priest branch

II. Society of missionaries, spread everywhere
   1. provide, help 2 poor
   2. undertake work, houses,
   3. Shut-ins, alchoholics, homeless
   4. MC, OIA, MAR 29 1963,
   5. Lay, Mother Theresa,
   6. Spirit, Charism

Virtues are the essence of the human spirit and the content of our character. Spend some time contemplating the following list of virtues. Do you suppose any of these virtues might be especially important in determining the strength of our character as we work together to build up God's Kingdom here on Earth? If you don't have a good definition for each of these virtues in your head and heart, then take some time to look up the definitions in your dictionary.

Key Virtues

acceptance	discernment	humility	peace	service
beauty	enthusiasm	idealism	perseverance	tolerance
cheerfulness	excellence	innocence	prayerfulness	trust
commitment	faith	integrity	purity	trustworthiness
compassion	flexibility	joy	purposefulness	trustfulness
confidence	forgiveness	justice	respect	unity
courage	generosity	kindness	responsibility	wisdom
courtesy	gentleness	love	reverence	wonder
creativity	grace	loyalty	righteousness	
detachment	gratitude	moderation	sacrifice	
devotion	hope	order	self-discipline	
diligence		patience		

Style Tools and Examples

Adverbs ending in "-ly" add to (and strengthen) verbs and give your writing power. Using sentence #1 as an example, choose one, two or three "-ly"s from the list on the next page for the blank spaces in sentences 2 through 5. Be sure to include a conjunction or a comma between your "-ly" words.

1. (Model) Mother Teresa **happily** received permission to start "The Missionaries of Charity", an organization that **cheerfully** loves **and bravely** cares for people that nobody else wants.

2. The Society of Missionaries has _anxiously_ spread all over the world, _miraculously_ including the former Soviet Union and Eastern European countries.

3. They _steadily_ but _simply_ provide effective help to the poorest of the poor in a number of countries.

4. The lay Missionaries of Charity try to _work humbly_ and _happily_ follow Mother Teresa's spirit and charism in their families.

5. Mother Teresa's work has been _quickly_ recognized and _cheerfully_ acclaimed throughout the world.

Adverbs: "-ly" Words

absolutely	finally	lightly	simply
anxiously	fortunately	masterfully	slowly
blindly	frantically	miraculously	steadily
bravely	frequently	mournfully	stubbornly
calmly	fundamentally	noisily	substantially
carefully	graciously	notably	successfully
certainly	gradually	occasionally	suddenly
cheerfully	happily	overly	surely
completely	heartily	predictably	tactfully
continually	heavenly	presumably	tenderly
conveniently	helpfully	primarily	terribly
critically	hopefully	probably	thoroughly
definitely	hopelessly	proudly	thoughtfully
diligently	humbly	quickly	tragically
distinctly	immediately	quietly	ultimately
divinely	impatiently	reasonably	unhappily
dramatically	inevitably	regularly	utterly
drastically	infinitely	repeatedly	violently
eagerly	instantly	sadly	virtually
easily	joyously	safely	willingly
energetically	kindly	separately	wistfully
evenly	knowingly	seriously	
eventually	laboriously	significantly	
faithfully	lazily	silently	

"-ly" Collection

Some people like to collect dolls, spoons, cards, bells or even bottle caps. Writers, however, love to collect words. Start right now collecting some "-ly" adverbs from your reading and other subject study. Start building a list on this page, and add to it throughout the year. You will find that a handy list of words is like a "brain expander" letting you skillfully use words you might never have thought of otherwise.

_____ _____ _____

_____ _____ _____

_____ _____ _____

_____ _____ _____

Unit II: Writing From Notes
Lesson 3: President Lincoln's Favorite Poem

Objective
To learn how to carefully limit notes and write a summary from them. To simplify this lesson, we will use only the first and fifth stanzas of the poem. Key words have already been underlined for you.

Source Text

> Oh, <u>why</u> should the spirit of <u>mortal</u> be <u>proud</u>?
> Like a <u>swift</u>-fleeting <u>meteor</u>, a fast-flying <u>cloud</u>,
> A flash of the <u>lightning</u>, a break of the <u>wave</u>,
> He <u>passes</u> from <u>life</u> to his <u>rest</u> in the grave.
>
> The leaves of the oak and the willow shall fade,
> Be scattered around, and together be laid;
> And the young and the old, the low and the high,
> Shall molder to dust, and together shall lie.
>
> The infant a mother attended and loved;
> The mother that infant's affection who proved;
> The husband, that mother and infant who blessed;
> Each, all, are away to their dwelling of rest.
>
> The maid on whose cheek, on whose brow, in whose eye,
> Shone beauty and pleasure - her triumphs are by;
> And the memory of those who loved her and praised,
> Are alike from the minds of the living erased.
>
> The <u>hand</u> of the <u>king</u> that the <u>sceptre</u> hath borne,
> The <u>brow</u> of the <u>priest</u> that the mitre hath <u>worn</u>,
> The <u>eye</u> of the <u>sage</u>, and the heart of the <u>brave</u>,
> Are hidden and <u>lost</u> in the depths of the <u>grave</u>.
>
> The peasant, whose lot was to sow and to reap,
> The herdsman, who climbed with his goats up the steep,
> The beggar, who wandered in search of his bread,
> Have faded away like the grass that we tread.
>
> The saint, who enjoyed the communion of Heaven,
> The sinner, who dared to remain unforgiven,
> The wise and the foolish, the guilty and just,
> Have quietly mingled their bones in the dust.
>
> So the <u>multitude</u> goes - like the flower or the weed

> That withers away to let others succeed;
> So the multitude comes - even those we behold,
> To repeat every tale that has often been told.
>
> For we are the same that our fathers have been;
> We see the same sights that our fathers have seen;
> We drink the same stream, we feel the same sun,
> And run the same course that our fathers have run.
>
> The thoughts we are thinking, our fathers would think;
> From the death we are shrinking, our fathers would shrink;
> To the life we are clinging, they also would cling -
> But it speeds from us all like a bird on the wing.
>
> They loved - but the story we cannot unfold;
> They scorned - but the heart of the haughty is cold;
> They grieved - but no wail from their slumber will come;
> They joyed - but the tongue of their gladness is dumb.
>
> They died - aye, they died - we things that are now,
> That walk on the turf that lies over their brow,
> And make in their dwellings a transient abode,
> Meet the things that they met on their pilgrimage road.
>
> Yea, hope and despondency, pleasure and pain,
> Are mingled together in sunshine and rain;
> And the smile and the tear, the song and the dirge,
> Still follow each other, like surge upon surge.
>
> 'Tis the wink of an eye - 'tis the draught of a breath -
> From the blossom of health to the paleness of death,
> From the gilded saloon to the bier and the shroud
> Oh, why should the spirit of mortal be proud?
>
> William Knox (1789-1825)

Assignment

1. Read the poem. The outline notes are carefully limited since the passages contain many details. (Remember, key words should reflect the main ideas of the sentence or verse, but you cannot choose all of the sentences or verses – just the most important ones.)
2. Following the outline, write one paragraph about the poem. Include all of the ideas from the outline in your paragraph, using the "Dress-ups" described on pages 17 & 18. Underline one of each of the dress-ups from your level. When you write your paragraph from the outline, write approximately one sentence per note. (For this assignment, there are 4 notes, so your paragraph should consist of approximately 4 sentences.)

3. Your first draft should be handwritten, double-spaced, with no erasing. Cross out any errors and write the corrections in the extra space above. Edit your first draft for spelling, punctuation and grammar as best you can, then have another person (parent, teacher or older sibling) check it as well. When it has been checked and corrected as thoroughly as possible, copy (or type) a final draft. Keep your final draft in this book with each lesson, or in the back separated with a divider.
4. Follow the checksheet on page 19. Your teacher may add (or delete) techniques you know (or don't know) to customize the checklist for your level of challenge. You must have at least one of each dress-up technique for each paragraph. As this assignment is only one paragraph, you will need at least one of each. (You may, of course have more than one "-ly" word, etc., but only underline one of each.)

Note Outline Model: President Lincoln's Favorite Poem
I. Why, mortal, proud
   1. Swift, meteor, cloud
   2. Lightning, wave
   3. Passes, life, rest

Style Tools and Examples
"who/which" clauses

From now on, each paragraph you write should contain at least one **adjective clause**, also called a **"who/which" clause**. These allow you to add detail or to connect ideas. Adjective clauses describe nouns and begin with *who, whom, whose,* or *which*. Everyone should complete the practice sentences below, following the first sentence as a model. Use *who* for people and *which* for things. Level B & C students must include a *who/which* in their composition for this lesson; Level A, in the next lesson.

1. (Model) Mortal man, **who should not be proud**, can become surprisingly haughty in a world **which has forgotten faith in God**.

2. The king, the priest and the sage <u>who</u> _____ could become angry <u>which</u> _____.

3. The peasant, the herdsman and beggar <u>who</u> _____ have faded away <u>which</u> _____.

4. In many ways we are the same as our fathers <u>who</u> _____ thought and feared that <u>which</u> _____.

5. For all things there is a time and a season, a time to hope and a time to despair, a time to smile and a time to cry, for those who _____ there will always be knowledge of new life to come which_____.

Invisible "who/which" clauses, Level C

In addition to a "who/which" clause (adjective) clause in every paragraph, Level C students should also put in an invisible "who/which" clause and mark it by underlining the words on either side of where the "which" would be, as shown in the model below. Always put a comma after the noun that precedes the invisible "who/which" clause.

(Visible who)   The king, who was raising his scepter, appeared glorious.
(Invisible who)   The king, raising his scepter, appeared glorious.
(Visible which)   The scepter, which a king once held high, is lost.
(Invisible which)   The scepter, a king once held high, is lost.

Style Note, Levels B & C

Avoid using *is, are, was,* or *were* as the main verb in a "who/which" clause, since they do not give the reader a strong picture of the subject of the sentence, as shown below.

The maid, who **was** for a time beautiful, is soon forgotten.
The grass, which **was** growing on the steep, is no longer lusciously vibrant.

Often, by changing the "who/which" clause to an invisible "who/which" clause, you can remove the weak verb without changing the sentence's meaning. Compare the following two sentences with the previous two.

The maid, **for a time beautiful**, is soon forgotten.
The grass, **growing on the steep**, is no longer lusciously vibrant.

Checksheet for Lesson 3

Levels A, B, & C

Presentation
___ title centered and underlined
___ name, date
___ clearly presented

Mechanics
___ indent paragraphs
___ complete sentences
___ capitals (uppercase)
___ punctuation

Style Tools
___ underline dress-ups (one of each)

Level A

Dress-Ups
"-ly" word ___

Level B

Dress-Ups
"-ly" word
"who/which" clause ___

Level C

Dress-Ups
dual "-ly" word ___
"who/which" clause ___
invisible "who/which" clause ___

Lesson 4: The Simplicity and Humility of St. Francis

Objective
To practice the skills of taking notes, creating note outlines, and writing summaries from the outlines.

Source Text

Simplicity
Francis's simple, childlike nature fastened on the thought, that if all are from one Father then all are real kin, hence his custom of claiming brotherhood with all manner of animate and inanimate objects. Francis's love of creatures was not simply the offspring of a soft or sentimental disposition; it arose rather from that deep and abiding sense of the presence of God, which underlies all he said and did. Even so, Francis's habitual cheerfulness was not that of a careless nature, or of one untouched by sorrow. None witnessed Francis's hidden struggles, his long agonies of tears, or his secret wrestling in prayer. And if we meet him making dumb-show of music, by playing a couple of sticks like a violin to give vent to his glee, we also find him heart-sore with foreboding at the dire dissensions in the order which threatened to make shipwreck of his ideal. Nor were temptations or other weakening maladies of the soul wanting to the saint at any time.

Humility
Humility was, no doubt, the saint's ruling virtue. The idol of an enthusiastic popular devotion, he ever truly believed himself less than the least. Equally admirable was Francis's prompt and docile obedience to the voice of grace within him, even in the early days of his ill-defined ambition, when the spirit of interpretation failed him. Later on, the saint, with as clear a sense of his message as any prophet ever had, yielded ungrudging submission to what constituted ecclesiastical authority. His apostolate embodied the very noblest spirit of reform; he strove to correct abuses by holding up an ideal.

Assignment
1. Read the source text.
2. In the space below, take notes for the two paragraphs. You will need to limit your notes, looking for the key words and key ideas very carefully.
3. After you have made your key word outline, verbally tell back the ideas represented by the key words to someone else. If you don't understand why you wrote the words you chose, go back and read the original text again.
4. Using the key words from your note outline, write a 2-paragraph composition entitled, "The Simplicity and Humility of St. Francis".

Double-space your first draft. Have it edited and then handwrite or type a final draft to keep in your folder.

Structural Tools and Suggestions

Whenever you make a note outline, follow the format below.
In the outline, Roman numerals indicate paragraph beginnings (and will later show topic sentences).
Make no more than 5 details per paragraph and 3 key words per detail.

Note Outline: The Simplicity and Humility of St. Francis

I. Simple, childlike
  1. one father claiming brotherhood
  2. Mother's presence of God
  3. cheerfulness long agonies
  4. of heartsore temptations
  5. weeping soul

II. Humility, virtue
  1. enthusiastic admirable
  2. voice of grace prompts
  3. obedience interpretation
  4. prophet authority

Style Tools and Examples
"because" clauses

Like the "who/which" clause, a "because" clause can be used to give more detail or to connect ideas. There is no special technique involved in using the word "because" in your paragraph, but you should be careful not to create a fragment. If you start your sentence with the word "because", then you will need to have a comma in that sentence. (Some teachers do not like sentences that start with "because", and if that's your situation, then you must not do it; try the word "since" or "as".)

1. (Model) St. Francis claimed brotherhood with all things **because all are from one Father.**

2. (Model) **Because Francis had a deep and abiding sense of the presence of God**, everything he said and did reflected this understanding.

3. One of Francis's virtues was cheerfulness <u>because</u> _____
   _____
   _____.

4. Francis wrestled with God in prayer <u>because</u> _____
   _____
   _____.

5. <u>Because</u> of dissensions in his order, _____
   _____
   _____.

Note the fragments, or incomplete sentences. Also, note the necessary commas in the correct example below.

1. Because of God's presence. (Incorrect)

2. Because of God's presence, St. Francis felt brotherhood with all animate and inanimate objects. (Correct)

Just for Fun
Look up St. Francis' "Canticle of the Sun" on the Internet or at your local public library. It's not very long and you can use it to expand your understanding of the mind of St. Francis. You can also use it to expand your writing for this assignment.

Checksheet for Lesson 4

Levels A, B, & C

Presentation
___ title centered and underlined
___ name, date
___ clearly presented

Mechanics
___ indent paragraphs
___ complete sentences
___ capitals (uppercase)
___ punctuation

Style Tools
___ underline dress-ups (one of each)

Paragraphs	I.	II.
Level A		
Dress-Ups		
"-ly" word	___	___
"who/which" clause	___	___
Level B		
Dress-Ups		
"-ly" word	___	___
"who/which" clause	___	___
"because" clause	___	___
Level C		
Dress-Ups		
dual "-ly" word	___	___
"who/which" clause	___	___
invisible "who/which" clause	___	___
(no "to be" verbs with "who/which")	___	___
"because" clause	___	___

Lesson 5: Abraham's Proclamations During the Civil War

Objective
To further practice the skills of taking notes, creating note outlines, and writing summaries from them. It is okay to break long sentences in this sample to create two lines of notes.

Source Text

God Prevails
"We are not enemies, but friends. We must not be enemies. Though passion may have strained it must not break our bonds of affection. The mystic chords of memory, stretching from every battlefield and patriot grave to every living heart and hearthstone all over this broad land, will yet swell the chorus of the Union, when again touched, as surely they will be, by the better angels of our nature."

"The will of God prevails. In great contests each party claims to act in accordance with the will of God. Both may be, and one must be, wrong. God cannot be for and against the same thing at the same time. In the present civil war it is quite possible that God's purpose is something different from the purpose of either party—and yet the human instrumentalities, working just as they do, are of the best adaptation to effect His purpose."

Thanksgiving
"We all declare for liberty; but in using the same word we do not all mean the same thing. With some the word liberty may mean for each man to do as he pleases with himself, and the product of his labor; while with others, the same word many mean for some men to do as they please with other men, and the product of other men's labor. Here are two, not only different, but incompatible things, called by the same name - liberty. And it follows that each of the things is, by the respective parties, called by two different and incompatible names—liberty and tyranny."

"I do therefore invite my fellow citizens in every part of the United States, and also those who are at sea and those who are sojourning in foreign lands, to set apart and observe the last Thursday of November next, as a day of Thanksgiving and Praise to our beneficent Father who dwelleth in the Heavens. And I recommend to them that while offering up the ascriptions justly due to Him for such singular deliverances and blessings, they do also, with humble penitence for our national perverseness and disobedience, commend to His tender care all those who have become widows, orphans, mourners or sufferers in the lamentable civil strife in which we are unavoidably engaged, and fervently implore the interposition of the Almighty Hand to heal the wounds of the nation and to restore it as soon as may be consistent with the Divine purposes to the full enjoyment of peace, harmony, tranquility and Union."

Assignment
1. Read the source text.
2. Take notes using the outline provided. Consider the quotes of the first two paragraphs of source text as one unit for the purposes of note taking. Consider the third and fourth paragraphs as a second unit.
3. Write a two-paragraph composition about the proclamations of President Lincoln during the Civil War (1861 – 1865).

Note Outline: Abraham's Proclamations During the Civil War

I. ⊘Enemies, Friends

1. must, not, enemies

2. passion, ⊘break, affection

3. chords, memory, battlefield→hearts

4. swell, Union, better nature

5. will, God prevails

6. both may, ① wrong

7. God, ⊘ for, ⊘ against, same

8. God's purpose, different, human instrumentalities

Style Tools and Examples
Quality Adjectives (Level B now, Level A later).
An adjective describes (or tells more about) a noun (person, place, thing or idea). For example, any word you write in the sentence below is probably an adjective. Try it with any of these words: mysterious, bright, blue, dangerous, thick, etc.

The _____ pen rolled off the _____ table.

Abraham raised the _____ knife to carve the turkey.

They found a _____ gift placed at their Thanksgiving feast.

Dual Adjectives, Level C
From now on, write at least one set of dual adjectives in every paragraph (and underline one set.) Dual adjectives modify the same noun, as in the example below.

    Wearily Abraham climbed the **steep, rugged** mountain.

Steep and *rugged* are dual adjectives describing *mountain*. Make sure that the two adjectives you use are not synonyms, as in: "Abraham had faith in his **precious, dear** Union".

Banned Adjectives
Some adjectives are "weak" or "cheap" in that they do not create a strong image or feeling for the reader. The words big, small, bad, good, and cool can easily be replaced by more descriptive choices. Refer to the Banned Adjectives list below to find alternatives to use in your compositions.

Add your own synonyms in the spaces provided. Use a thesaurus or keep a list of words found in your reading.

big	**small**	**bad**	**good**	**cool**
sizable	tiny	lousy	great	interesting
gigantic	miniscule	wicked	fantastic	captivating
huge	petite	unpleasant	admirable	superb
enormous	slight	horrible	pleasant	excellent
immense	puny	terrible	wholesome	awesome
massive	trivial	evil	noble	stupendous
grand	minor	awful	wonderful	stylish
_____	_____	_____	_____	_____
_____	_____	_____	_____	_____
_____	_____	_____	_____	_____
_____	_____	_____	_____	_____
_____	_____	_____	_____	_____
_____	_____	_____	_____	_____
_____	_____	_____	_____	_____

Just for Fun

In 1621 the Plymouth colonists and the Wampanoag Indians shared an autumn harvest feast which is now known as the first Thanksgiving. On November 1, 1782 the date for Thanksgiving was set on November 28th. Why was the date changed later and who changed it?

Checksheet for Lesson 5

Levels A, B, & C	Paragraphs	I.	II.
Presentation ___ title centered and underlined ___ name, date ___ clearly presented **Mechanics** ___ indent paragraphs ___ complete sentences ___ capitals (uppercase) ___ punctuation **Style Tools** ___ underline dress-ups (one of each) ___ no "banned" adjectives	**Level A** **Dress-Ups** "-ly" word "who/which" clause "because" clause	___ ___ ___	___ ___ ___
	Level B **Dress-Ups** "-ly" word "who/which" clause "because" clause quality adjective	___ ___ ___ ___	___ ___ ___ ___
	Level C **Dress-Ups** dual "-ly" word "who/which" clause invisible "who/which" clause (no "to be" verbs with "who/which") "because" clause dual adjectives	___ ___ ___ ___ ___	___ ___ ___ ___ ___

Unit III: Summarizing Narrative Stories
Lesson 6: Mother Teresa Speaks on Abortion

Objective
To learn how to summarize narrative stories, a step toward reviewing and critiquing books and movies. In Unit III, you will create outlines primarily by following your level of the Narrative Story Model. This system of creating outlines will be useful when you summarize long or short stories, books or movies, plays, videos or speeches (such as the following excerpt from Mother Teresa's Nobel Lecture during her receipt of the Nobel Peace Prize in Oslo, Norway on December 11, 1979). In each case you follow a 3-paragraph Narrative Story Model.

Source Text

"I was surprised in the West to see so many young boys and girls given into drugs, and I tried to find out why—why is it like that, and the answer was: because there is no one in the family to receive them. Father and mother are so busy they have no time. Young parents are in some institution and the child takes back to the street and gets involved in something. We are talking of peace. These are things that break peace, but I feel the greatest destroyer of peace today is abortion, because it is a direct war, a direct killing—direct murder by the mother herself. And we read in the Scripture, for God says very clearly: Even if a mother could forget her child—I will not forget you—I have carried you in the palm of My hand. We are carried in the palm of His hand, so close to Him that unborn child has been carried in the hand of God. And that is what strikes me most, the beginning of that sentence, that even if a mother could forget something—impossible—but even if she could forget—I will not forget you. And today the greatest means—the greatest destroyer of peace is abortion. And we who are standing here—our parents wanted us. We would not be here if our parents would do that to us. Our children, we want them, we love them, but what of the millions".

"Many people are very, very concerned with the children in India, with the children in Africa where quite a number die, maybe of malnutrition, of hunger and so on, but millions are dying deliberately by the will of the mother. And this is what is the greatest destroyer of peace today. Because if a mother can kill her own child, what is left for me to kill you and you to kill me? There is nothing between. And this I appeal in India, I appeal everywhere: Let us bring the child back, and this year being the child's year: What have we done for the child? At the beginning of the year I told, I spoke everywhere and I said: Let us make this the year that we make every single child born, and unborn, wanted. And today is the end of the year, have we really made the children wanted? I will give you something terrifying. We are fighting abortion by adoption, we have saved thousands of lives, we have sent words to all the clinics, to the hospitals, police stations—please don't destroy the child, we will take the child. So every hour of the day and night it is always somebody, we have quite a number of unwedded mothers—tell them come, we will take care of you, we will take the child from you, and we will get a home for the child. And we have a tremendous demand from families who have no children that is the blessing of God for us".

"And also, we are doing another thing that is very beautiful—we are teaching our beggars, our leprosy patients, our slum dwellers, and our people of the street, natural family planning. In Calcutta alone in six years—it is all in Calcutta—we have had 61,273 babies less from the families who would have had, but because they practice this natural way of abstaining, of self-control, out of love for each other. We teach them the temperature meter, which is very beautiful, very simple, and our poor people understand. And you know what they have told me? Our family is healthy, our family is united, and we can have a baby whenever we want. So clear—those people in the street, those beggars—and I think that if our people can do like that how much more you and all the others who can know the ways and means without destroying the life that God has created in us".

Assignment
1. Read the source text. The Narrative Story Model found on the following page has been adjusted for Levels A-C. The forms are very similar, and all lead to the same result.
2. The first paragraph of a 3-paragraph composition appears on the next page. Using the Narrative Story Model Outline as a guide, write the other two paragraphs, following the checklist on page 34.
3. Save your work as we will revisit this narrative model and critique process in Unit IX.

Structural Tools and Suggestions
This outline format is different from the one you learned in Units I and II. Rather than taking key words from the source text, use the story sequence chart to ask yourself questions about the story. Put the answers in a three-paragraph outline format. The information you put in your outline may not be in the same order as it appears on the original story. Paragraphs should be of approximately equal length. In the last sentence of your last paragraph, include 2-3 key words that also appear in your composition's title. You may wish to wait until writing the last paragraph to decide the title. Your title should repeat the key words of the last sentence.

Narrative Story Model Note Outline: Mother Teresa Speaks on Abortion

Story Sequence Chart
3 Forms of the Same Model

Outline	A	B	C

I. West, young people, drugs
   1. parents, absent, busy
   2. young parents, prison
   3. kids, gangs
   4. peace, broken
   5. children, not wanted
 	
II. abortion, greatest destroyer
   1. murder, mother
   2. God, holds all
   3. India, Africa, too many
   4. Year of Child, adoption
   5. clinics, hospitals
 	
III. poor people, NFP
   1. Calcutta, 61,273 less
   2. self-control, love
   3. thermometer, simple
   4. poor, understand
   5. rich, understand?
	I.
	Who is in the story?
	What are they like?
	Where did they live?
	What was their situation?
	When did they live?
		I.
		Who?
		Like?
		Where?
		When?
		Mood?
			I.
			Characters
			Setting
			(Time & Place)
			Mood

	II. What was the problem? What happened? What did they think? What did they say? What did they do?	II. Problem? What happened? Think? Say? Do?	II. Conflict Plot
	III. Climax? How was the problem solved? How could the problem be solved? What is the moral message?	III. Climax? Solution? Moral? Message?	III. Climax Theme Message

Title Repeats Key Words of Last Sentence

Model First Paragraph: Mother Teresa Speaks on Abortion

The first week of December 1979, Mother Teresa traveled from Calcutta, India to Oslo, Norway so that she could accept the Nobel Peace Prize of 1979. On December 11th, she delivered a speech, as all recipients are expected to do. During her lecture, she pointed out that drug use among young people in the West seems to be very normal. By "West", she meant the advanced, industrialized nations like the United States of America. Mother Teresa pointed out that children might turn to drugs if they feel unwanted by their parents. Many times parents are too young themselves and may be using drugs and may end up in prison. Then who cares for the children? Probably, gangs continue to grow in the United States because of this sad situation. Peace is broken where children are not wanted. Jesus said, "Let the children come to me and do not prevent them; for the kingdom of God belongs to such as these." (Luke 18:16) Like Jesus, Mother Teresa says, "Tell them come, we will take care of you, we will take the child from you, and we will get a home for the child."	who? characters? where? - place when? - time

Style Tools and Examples (Level B & C now, Level A later)

The next dress-up element is an adverbial clause, which begins with one of the clausal starters shown here. In each paragraph you write from now on, include and underline an adverb clause that begins with one of these clausal starters. "Because" can also be an adverbial starter, although you will use the "because" along with another clause for several more lessons. Note that the first letter of the words: *when, while, where, as, since, if, although,* when said in that order, can create the Web site-looking acronym "www.asia"

> **ADVERBIAL CLAUSAL STARTERS:**
> *when while where as since if although (because)*

She inquired of her assistants… <u>when</u> they gathered together.
<u>while</u> dinner was served.
<u>where</u> they would feel at ease.
<u>as</u> soon as she arrived in Oslo.
<u>since</u> they had the keys to her suitcase.
as <u>if</u> she expected good news from them.
<u>although</u> she was exhausted from her trip.
<u>because</u> the prize was at stake.

Practice creating adverbial clauses with the following examples. Ask your parent or teacher for suggestions if you can't think of anything. If you can't write small enough to fit your clause on one line, use a blank paper instead. (This applies to any of the fill-in-the-blank exercises in this book.)

Mother Teresa invested the Nobel Peace Prize money wisely…

when _____.

while _____.

where _____.

as _____.

since _____.

if _____.

although _____.

She took from the lazy assistant the responsibility he had been given…

when _____.

while _____.

where _____.

as _____.

since _____.

if _____.

although _____.

33

Checksheet for Lesson 6

Levels A, B, & C

Presentation
___ title centered and underlined
___ name, date
___ clearly presented

Mechanics
___ indent paragraphs
___ complete sentences
___ capitals (uppercase)
___ punctuation

Structure
___ follows model
___ paragraphs roughly equal size
___ title reflects key words of last sentence

Style Tools
___ underline dress-ups (one of each)
___ no "banned" adjectives

Paragraphs   I.   II.

Level A

   Dress-Ups
   "-ly" word   ___ ___
   "who/which" clause   ___ ___
   "because" clause   ___ ___
   quality adjective   ___ ___

Level B

   Dress-Ups
   "-ly" word   ___ ___
   "who/which" clause   ___ ___
   (no "to be" verbs with "who/which")
   "because" clause   ___ ___
   quality adjective   ___ ___
   adverbial clause (www.asia)   ___ ___

Level C

   Dress-Ups
   dual "-ly" word   ___ ___
   "who/which" clause   ___ ___
   invisible "who/which" clause   ___ ___
   (no "to be" verbs with "who/which")
   "because" clause   ___ ___
   dual adjectives   ___ ___
   adverbial clause (www.asia)   ___ ___

Lesson 7: Abraham and the Town Bully

Objective
To practice summarizing narrative stories using Abe's story of virtue found in new friendship and the repression of violence.

Source Text

Abraham Lincoln moved to New Salem, Illinois, in 1831. The Clary's Grove boys lived in a settlement near New Salem. They were a loud, reckless, frontier crowd. They boasted they could wrestle better than any group throughout Illinois. At times they could also be generous and good-natured. Their leader was a man named Jack Armstrong.

Denton Offutt, in whose store Lincoln was a clerk, bragged that his employee was mentally and physically superior to any of the Clary's Grove boys. He openly said Lincoln could whip any man in the community. Hearing of Offutt's boasting, Jack Armstrong challenged Lincoln to a wrestling match. Lincoln accepted.

The entire town turned out for the fight. Offutt bet $10 Lincoln would win. Other residents wagered money and trinkets. Lincoln was 6' 4" and weighed 185 pounds, but Jack Armstrong was an experienced, formidable opponent. Although he was smaller than Lincoln, he was strong as an ox. The stage was set.

For a time, the two scufflers circled each other warily. They did some grappling and twisting, but neither man was able to throw the other to the ground. Slowly, Armstrong began to get the worst of it. Finally, Lincoln grabbed the bully by the neck, held him at arm's length, and shook him like a little boy. This aroused the Clary's Grove boys, and it suddenly appeared that the entire crowd of people could attack Abe. He backed up against the wall of Offutt's store and offered to take them on one at a time.

Jack Armstrong was impressed with Abraham's display of courage. He came forward, took Lincoln's hand and shook it heartily. He looked at his friends and said, "Boys, Abe Lincoln is the best fellow that ever broke into this settlement. He shall be one of us." From then on, Abraham Lincoln and Jack Armstrong were the best of friends! Abraham had a calming influence on the whole gang of Clary's Grove boys, and his charisma had the effect of repressing their violence.

Later, Jack and his wife, Hannah, allowed Lincoln to stay in their home when he was periodically out of work. Abraham returned the favor in 1858 when Bill Armstrong, son of Jack and Hannah, was falsely accused of murder. Lincoln was the defense attorney, and the jury returned a not guilty verdict. After the trial, when the topic of Lincoln's fee arose, Abraham said, "Why, Hannah, I shan't charge you a cent, never. Anything I can do for you I will do willingly and without charges."

Assignment
1. Read the source text.
2. Construct a 3-paragraph outline which follows the Narrative Story Model, by asking questions about the story from the Story Sequence Chart. (Use 3-5 details per paragraph)
3. From your outline, write a double-spaced, 3-paragraph composition.
4. Proofread your composition, making sure you included all the elements of presentation, structure, mechanics, and style. Get a second opinion if possible. When you are satisfied, prepare a final draft.

Structural Tools and Suggestions
You may limit details in each paragraph, including only 3 or 4 details in one, perhaps 5 in another.

When written out, paragraphs should be approximately the same size to keep your composition balanced, and each paragraph should be at least four sentences long.

If the story is short on details, imagine what the characters might have been thinking, feeling, or saying, and add in some content that complements the story. For example, in this story of Honest Abe as a young man, you might include some dialog such as: *When Mr. Offutt had left the store, one clerk commented, "Since Abe is fighting tomorrow, I think I'll go fishing tonight so I've got something to wager."*

Narrative Story Model Outline: Abraham and the Town Bully

I. Abraham, moved, New Salem	
1. _____	◆Who is in the story?
2. _____	◆What were they like?
3. _____	◆Where did they go?
4. _____	◆When did the action occur?
5. _____	
II. Entire town, fight, wagers	
1. _____	◆What was the problem?
2. _____	◆What happened?

3. _____
 4. _____
 5. _____
 III. Abe's courage, Jack's friendship, retribution
  1. _____
  2. _____
  3. _____
  4. _____
  5. _____
	◆What did they think?
	 ◆What did they say?
	 ◆What did they do?
	
	 ◆Climax
	 ◆How was the problem solved?
	 ◆What is the moral message?
	 ◆Title repeats key words from last sentence.

Style Tools and Example (Level B & C now, Level A later)
Strong Verbs

Strengthen your writing by using powerful verbs rather than "weak" ones. Examine the sentences below as they progress from weak and ordinary to powerful.

1. (ordinary verb) He **knocked** on the door.
2. (more powerful verb) He **pounded** on the door.
3. (with an adverb added) He **vigorously pounded** on the door.
4. (dual power verbs) He **vigorously pounded and kicked** the door.
5. (dual "-ly"s and dual verbs) He **loudly and violently pounded on and kicked** the door.

Dual Verbs, Level C

From now on, write dual verbs into each paragraph to strengthen your compositions. Note the conjunctions – *and, even, then,* and *but*.

He was invited to **and** joined in the wedding feast.
The bird chirped **even** warbled before dawn.
She inspected **then** purchased the house.
She sang **but** faltered half way through.

Triple Verbs, Advanced (optional)
For advanced students, include at least one set of triple verbs in each paragraph of your compositions.

The clerks **hoisted, tipped, and poured** the molasses jars empty.
Kites **glided, dipped, and soared** in the midday sky.

Banned Verbs
Add your own synonyms in the spaces provided.

go/went	see/saw	say/said	eat/ate	think/thought
travel/ed	notice/d	yell/ed	gobble/d	ponder/ed
journey/ed	eye/d	whisper/ed	devour/ed	believe/d
wander/ed	peer/ed	command/ed	munch/ed	imagine/d
run/ran	glimpse/d	ask/ed	slurp/ed	remember/ed

Checksheet for Lesson 7

Levels A, B, & C

Presentation
___ title centered and underlined
___ name, date
___ clearly presented

Mechanics
___ indent paragraphs
___ complete sentences
___ capitals (uppercase)
___ punctuation

Structure
___ follows model
___ paragraphs roughly equal size
___ title reflects key words of last sentence

Style Tools
___ underline dress-ups (one of each)
___ no "banned" adjectives
___ no "banned" verbs (B & C only)

Paragraphs	I.	II.	III.

Level A

Dress-Ups
"-ly" word ___ ___ ___
"who/which" clause ___ ___ ___
"because" clause ___ ___ ___
quality adjective ___ ___ ___

Level B

Dress-Ups
"-ly" word ___ ___ ___
"who/which" clause
(no "to be" verbs with
"who/which") ___ ___ ___
"because" clause ___ ___ ___
quality adjective ___ ___ ___
adverbial clause
(www.asia) ___ ___ ___
strong verb ___ ___ ___

Level C

Dress-Ups
dual "-ly" word ___ ___ ___
"who/which" clause ___ ___ ___
invisible "who/which"
clause
(no "to be" verbs with
"who/which") ___ ___ ___
"because" clause ___ ___ ___
dual adjectives ___ ___ ___
adverbial clause
(www.asia) ___ ___ ___
dual (or triple) verbs ___ ___ ___

Lesson 8: St. Francis and the Animals

Objective
To practice summarizing. In this lesson, limiting becomes important because you will summarize a much longer story.

Source Text

One day a brother brought a rabbit who had been caught in a trap to St. Francis. Francis advised the rabbit to be more alert in the future, then released the rabbit from the trap and set it on the ground to go its way. But the rabbit hopped back up onto Francis' lap, desiring to be close to the saint.

Francis took the rabbit a few steps into the woods and set it down. But it followed Francis back to his seat and hopped on his lap again! Finally Francis asked one of his fellow friars to take the rabbit far into the woods and let it go. That worked. This type of thing happened repeatedly to Francis—which he saw as an opportunity to praise the glory of God. If the simplest creatures could be so endowed with God's wonder, how much the more so we humans!

On another occasion, Father Francis and his companions were making a trip through the Spoleto Valley near the town of Bevagna. Suddenly, Francis spotted a great number of birds of all varieties. There were doves, crows and all sorts of birds. Swept up in the moment, Francis left his friends in the road and ran after the birds, who patiently waited for him. He greeted them in his usual way, expecting them to scurry off into the air as he spoke. But they moved not.

Filled with awe, he asked them if they would stay awhile and listen to the Word of God. He said to them: "My brother and sister birds, you should praise your Creator and always love him: He gave you feathers for clothes, wings to fly and all other things that you need. It is God who made you noble among all creatures, making your home in thin, pure air. Without sowing or reaping, you receive God's guidance and protection."

At this the birds began to spread their wings, stretch their necks and gaze at Francis, rejoicing and praising God in a wonderful way according to their nature. Francis then walked right through the middle of them, turned around and came back, touching their heads and bodies with his tunic. Then he gave them his blessing, making the Sign of the Cross over them. At that they flew off and Francis, rejoicing and giving thanks to God, went on his way.

Later, Francis wondered aloud to his companions why he had never preached to birds before. And from that day on, Francis made it his habit to solicitously invoke all birds, all animals and reptiles to praise and love their Creator.

Perhaps the most famous story of St. Francis is when he tamed the wolf that was terrorizing the people of Gubbio. While Francis was staying in that town he learned of a wolf so ravenous that it was not only killing and eating animals, but people, too. The people took up arms and went after it, but those who encountered the wolf perished at its sharp teeth. Villagers became afraid to leave the city walls.

Francis had pity on the people and decided to go out and meet the wolf. The people desperately warned him, but he insisted that God would take care of him. A brave friar and several peasants accompanied Francis outside the city gate. But soon the peasants lost heart and said they would go no farther.

Francis and his companion began to walk on. Suddenly the wolf, jaws agape, charged out of the woods at the couple. Francis made the Sign of the Cross toward it. The power of God caused the wolf to slow down and to close its mouth.

Then Francis called out to the creature: "Come to me, Brother Wolf. In the name of Christ, I order you not to hurt anyone." At that moment the wolf lowered its head and lay down at St. Francis' feet, meek as a lamb.

St. Francis explained to the wolf that he had been terrorizing the people, killing not only animals, but humans who are made in the image of God. "Brother Wolf," said Francis, "I want to make peace between you and the people of Gubbio. They will harm you no more and you must no longer harm them. All past crimes are to be forgiven."

The wolf showed its assent by moving its body and nodding its head. Then to the absolute surprise of the gathering crowd, Francis asked the wolf to make a pledge. As St. Francis extended his hand to receive the pledge, the wolf extended its front paw and placed it into the saint's hand. Then Francis commanded the wolf to follow him into town to make a peace pact with the townspeople. The wolf meekly followed St. Francis.

By the time they got to the town square, everyone was there to witness the miracle. With the wolf at his side, Francis gave the town a sermon on the wondrous and fearful love of God, calling them to repent from all their sins. Then he offered the townspeople peace, on behalf of the wolf. The townspeople promised in a loud voice to feed the wolf. Then Francis asked the wolf if he would live in peace under those terms. He bowed his head and twisted his body in a way that convinced everyone he accepted the pact. Then once again the wolf placed its paw in Francis' hand as a sign of the pact.

From that day on the people kept the pact they had made. The wolf lived for two years among the townspeople, going from door to door for food. It hurt no one and no one hurt it. Even the dogs did not bark at it. When the wolf finally died of old age, the people of Gubbio were sad. The wolf's peaceful ways had been a living reminder to them of the wonders, patience, virtues and holiness of St. Francis.

Assignment
1. Read the source text.
2. Create a 3-paragraph outline, carefully following the Narrative Story Model given in Lesson 6, by asking questions from the Story Sequence Chart. Handwrite your outline into the space provided below.
3. Following your outline & checksheet, write a 3-paragraph, double-spaced summary from your outline. Edit, get help, and when you are satisfied, rewrite or type your composition.

Structural Tools and Suggestions
Don't forget to balance your composition. In the conclusion, you are welcome to comment on what the moral or message of this story might be. Remember to use dramatic words from your last sentence to create a title that grabs the reader's attention.

Narrative Story Model Outline: St. Francis and the Animals

I. _____
    1. _____
    2. _____
    3. _____
    4. _____
    5. _____
	◆Who is in the story?
	 ◆What were they like?
	 ◆Where did they go?
	 ◆When did the action occur?

II. _____
    1. _____
    2. _____
    3. _____
    4. _____
    5. _____
	◆What was the problem?
	 ◆What happened?
	 ◆What did they think?
	 ◆What did they say?
	 ◆What did they do?

III. _____
 	
    1. _____
 	
    2. _____
 	
    3. _____
 	
    4. _____
 	
    5. _____
	♦Climax
	♦How was the problem solved?
	♦What is the moral message?
	♦Title repeats key words from last sentence.

Possible Adjectives

Checksheet for Lesson 8

Levels A, B, & C

Presentation
___ title centered and underlined
___ name, date
___ clearly presented

Mechanics
___ indent paragraphs
___ complete sentences
___ capitals (uppercase)
___ punctuation

Structure
___ follows model
___ paragraphs roughly equal size
___ title reflects key words of last sentence

Style Tools
___ underline dress-ups (one of each)
___ no "banned" adjectives
___ no "banned" verbs (B & C only)

Paragraphs	I.	II.	III.

Level A

Dress-Ups
"-ly" word ___ ___ ___
"who/which" clause ___ ___ ___
"because" clause ___ ___ ___
quality adjective ___ ___ ___

Level B

Dress-Ups
"-ly" word ___ ___ ___
"who/which" clause
 (no "to be" verbs with "who/which") ___ ___ ___
"because" clause ___ ___ ___
quality adjective ___ ___ ___
adverbial clause
(www.asia) ___ ___ ___
strong verb ___ ___ ___

Level C

Dress-Ups
dual "-ly" word ___ ___ ___
"who/which" clause ___ ___ ___
invisible "who/which" clause ___ ___ ___
(no "to be" verbs with "who/which")
"because" clause ___ ___ ___
dual adjectives ___ ___ ___
adverbial clause
(www.asia) ___ ___ ___
dual (or triple) verbs ___ ___ ___

Lesson 9: Mother's Shoes are Hard to Fill

Objective
To learn to rewrite narrative stories, using the plot of the Sunil Das saga but changing the characters and setting.

Source Text

Sixteen-year-old Sunil Das used to work in a roadside eating place at Halisahar, about 50 km north of Calcutta. About a month ago when his legs showed symptoms of leprosy, his employer sent him home. But the boy's stepmother would not keep him with the family and his father, a construction worker, pleaded helplessness. He was brought to the Gandhiji Prem Nivas, a center for leprosy patients run by the Missionaries of Charity at Titagarh. Last Tuesday, Sunil was to be released as his legs had improved but he pleaded with Brother Eugene, the man in charge of the center, to let him stay in the adjoining hostel.

"I won't go back home because my stepmother never loved me. Now that I had this disease, they won't take me back. I'm much better here." Sunil who never went to school had not heard of Mother Teresa until recently. "We were told she loved people like us, the poor and the sick, whom nobody loved and cared for."

Sunil's story has been the quintessential saga of Mother Teresa and her Missionaries of Charity since 1950 when the Albanian-born nun set up the religious order in Calcutta.

Carrying on the legacy of Mother Teresa, whom the world has known as the "Saint of the Gutters" and the "Apostle of the Unwanted", is not an easy task. No one knows this better than Sister Nirmala, the 65-year-old Nepali-born nun who replaced Mother Teresa six months before her death. The transformation has been particularly dramatic for the low-profile nun because she had spent seven years in the seclusion of the order's contemplative wing before being hoisted onto the center stage. But the job seems to have changed the nun substantially, making her articulate and composed.

Assignment
1. Read the Source Text.
2. Create a 3-paragraph outline following the Narrative Story Model. Keep to a maximum of five details per paragraph. Limiting is vital.
3. Using your outline, write a double-spaced, 3-paragraph composition, describing the story of Sunil Das. Use your checksheet to make sure you include all the required elements, have it edited, then rewrite or type a final version.

4. Change the characters and setting but keep the problem. For example, instead of happening in India, your story could take place in your very own hometown. This might change where the son (or daughter) would work, what kind of disease he (or she) might have contracted, and it might change the type of desperate situation he or she would come to. You or your mother or father could be Mother Teresa or Sister Nirmala. This technique of changing characters and setting but keeping the basic plot can be used for creative writing practice with almost any story, as well as with fables or fairy tales.

Narrative Story Outline: Mother's Shoes are Hard to Fill

I. _____

    1. _____

    2. _____

    3. _____

    4. _____

    5. _____

II. _____

    1. _____

    2. _____

    3. _____

    4. _____

    5. _____

III. _____

    1. _____

    2. _____

    3. _____

> 4. _____
>
> 5. _____

Style Tools and Examples (Level B & C)
Sentence Openers, Part 1

Using the six sentence openers taught in this book, you can improve the flow of your writing and add variety to your paragraphs. As you learn each opener, include it in every paragraph you write and indicate it by placing its number (found below) in the margin. Here are the first three:

❶ **Subject openers** begin with nouns, pronouns or the articles *a*, *an*, and *the*. (Subject openers are the most common openers, so they should be very easy to use.)

noun:	**Sagas** are stories about real people's challenges.
pronoun:	**He** never forgot his son, who had been forced to leave.
The:	**The** son begged his father for help.
A/an:	**A** sumptuous feast awaited him.

❷ **Prepositional openers:** Any preposition can be used in a prepositional opener:

Near the ocean	**With** her mother	**After** the storm	**Among** friends
Inside the palace	**In** the beginning	**On** the third day	**At** once

❸ **"-ly" or adverb openers:** When using an "-ly" word as a dress-up, it comes in the middle of sentences. Here "-ly" words are openers:

> **Angrily** the stepmother rejected her son.
> **Lovingly** the Brother welcomed him to stay.

Note: This "-ly" opener does not count as the "-ly" dress-up; from now on you'll have at least two "-ly" words in each paragraph: one in the middle (or at the end) of a sentence and one as the first word in a sentence.

Practice: Rewrite the #1 sentence below as a #2 (prepositional) opener, and as a #3 (ly) opener:

❶ The father was angry about his son's disease and refused to participate.

❷ *With his stepmother,* _____.

❸ *Angrily,* _____.

47

Prepositions

about	aside from	beyond	inside	opposite	toward
above	at	by	instead	out	under
according to	away from	concerning	into	outside	underneath
across	because of	despite	like	over	unlike
after	before	down	minus	past	until
against	behind	during	near	regarding	up
along	below	except	of	since	upon
amid	beneath	for	off	through	with
among	beside	from	on	throughout	within
around	between	in	onto	to	without

More Practice: Rewrite the #1 sentence below as a #2 (prepositional) opener, and as a #3 (ly) opener:

❶ The boy finally found a job with a farmer.

❷ _____.

❸ _____.

❶ The Brother was happy to assist many young people.

❷ _____.

❸ _____.

❶ The Sister felt great love in her heart.

❷ _____.

❸ _____.

❶ The boy was completely healed.

❷ _____.

❸ _____.

Checksheet for Lesson 9

Levels A, B, & C

Presentation
___ title centered and underlined
___ name, date
___ clearly presented

Mechanics
___ indent paragraphs
___ complete sentences
___ capitals (uppercase)
___ punctuation

Structure
___ follows model
___ paragraphs roughly equal size
___ title reflects key words of last sentence

Style Tools
___ underline dress-ups (one of each)
___ no "banned" adjectives
___ no "banned" verbs
___ put sentence opener numbers in the margins (B & C only)

Sentence Openers (B & C only)
(Use all three in each paragraph)
___ ❶ subject
___ ❷ preposition
___ ❸ "-ly" word

Paragraphs   I.   II.   III.

Level A

Dress-Ups
"-ly" word   ___ ___ ___
"who/which" clause   ___ ___ ___
"because" clause   ___ ___ ___
quality adjective   ___ ___ ___
adverbial clause
(www.asia)   ___ ___ ___

Level B

Dress-Ups
"-ly" word   ___ ___ ___
"who/which" clause
(no "to be" verbs with
"who/which")   ___ ___ ___
"because" clause   ___ ___ ___
quality adjective   ___ ___ ___
adverbial clause
(www.asia)   ___ ___ ___
strong verb   ___ ___ ___
sentence openers   ___ ___ ___

Level C

Dress-Ups
dual "-ly" word   ___ ___ ___
"who/which" clause   ___ ___ ___
invisible "who/which" clause
(no "to be" verbs with
"who/which")   ___ ___ ___
"because" clause   ___ ___ ___
dual adjectives
adverbial clause
(www.asia)   ___ ___ ___
dual (or triple) verbs   ___ ___ ___
sentence openers   ___ ___ ___

Unit IV: Summarizing References
Lesson 10: Abraham Speaks on Temperance

Objective
To learn to take notes and create an outline for reference from academic material. As always, the main goal is to rewrite the materials in your own words using only your notes. Note taking from references does not follow the model used in Unit III. Instead, it is like the system described in Units II and I with even greater limiting. Also, you will learn to organize facts into paragraphs using the topic/clincher model. The following source material is extremely difficult. Take your time with it and get help from your teacher if you don't understand some part or parts. Please note the three sections of the address.

Source Text

Abraham Lincoln's, "Address on Temperance," 22 February 1842 (edited)

I.

Although the temperance cause has been in progress for near twenty years, it is apparent to all that it is just now being crowned with a degree of success hitherto unparalleled. The list of its friends is daily swelled by the additions of fifties, of hundreds, and of thousands. The cause itself seems suddenly transformed from a cold abstract theory to a living, breathing, active, and powerful chieftain, going forth "conquering and to conquer." The citadels of his great adversary are daily being stormed and dismantled; his temple and his altars, where the rites of his idolatrous worship have long been performed, and where human sacrifices have long been wont to be made, are daily desecrated and deserted. The triumph of the conqueror's fame is sounding from hill to hill, from sea to sea, and from land to land, and calling millions to his standard at a blast.

For this new and splendid success we heartily rejoice. That this success is so much greater now than heretofore is doubtless owing to rational causes; and if we would have it continue, we shall do well to inquire what those causes are. The warfare heretofore waged against the demon intemperance has somehow or other been erroneous. Either the champions engaged or the tactics they adopted have not been the most proper. These champions for the most part have been preachers, lawyers, and hired agents. Between these and the mass of mankind there is a want of approachability, if the term be admissible, partially, at least, fatal to their success. They are supposed to have no sympathy of feeling or interest with those very persons whom it is their object to convince and persuade.

And again, it is so common and so easy to ascribe motives to men of these classes other than those they profess to act upon. The preacher, it is said, advocates temperance because he is a fanatic, and desires a union of the church and state; the lawyer from his pride and vanity of hearing himself speak; and the hired agent for his salary. But when one who has long been known as a victim of intemperance bursts the fetters that have bound him, and appears before his neighbors "clothed and in his right mind", a redeemed specimen of long-lost humanity, and stands up, with tears of joy trembling in his eyes, to tell of the miseries once endured, now to be endured no more forever; of his once naked and starving children, now clad and fed comfortably; of a wife long weighed down with woe, weeping, and a broken heart, now restored to health, happiness, and a renewed affection; and how easily it is all done, once it is resolved to be done; how simple his language! There is a logic and an eloquence in it that few with human feelings can resist. They cannot say that he desires a union of church and state, for he is not a church member; they cannot say he is vain of hearing himself speak, for his whole demeanor shows he would gladly avoid speaking at all; they cannot say he speaks for pay, for he receives none, and asks for none. Nor can his sincerity in any way be doubted, or his sympathy for those he would persuade to imitate his example be denied.

In my judgment, it is to the battles of this new class of champions that our late success is greatly, perhaps chiefly, owing. But, had the old-school champions themselves been of the most wise selecting, was their system of tactics the most judicious? It seems to me it was not. Too much denunciation against dram-sellers and dram-drinkers was indulged in. This I think was both impolitic and unjust. It was impolitic, because it is not much in the nature of man to be driven to anything; still less to be driven about that which is exclusively his own business; and least of all where such driving is to be submitted to at the expense of pecuniary interest or burning appetite. When the dram-seller and drinker were incessantly told—not in accents of entreaty and persuasion, diffidently addressed by erring man to an erring brother, but in the thundering tones of anathema and denunciation with which the lordly judge often groups together all the crimes of the felon's life, and thrusts them in his face just ere he passes sentence of death upon him—that they were the authors of all the vice and misery and crime in the land; that they were the manufacturers and material of all the thieves and robbers and murderers that infest the earth; that their houses were the workshops of the devil; and that their persons should be shunned by all the good and virtuous, as moral pestilences—I say, when they were told all this, and in this way, it is not wonderful that they were slow, very slow, to acknowledge the truth of such denunciations, and to join the ranks of their denouncers in a hue and cry against themselves.

II.

To have expected them to do otherwise than they did—to have expected them not to meet denunciation with denunciation, crimination with crimination, and anathema with anathema—was to expect a reversal of human nature, which is God's decree and can never be reversed. When the conduct of men is designed to be influenced, persuasion, kind, unassuming persuasion, should ever be adopted. It is an old and a true maxim "that a drop of honey catches more flies than a gallon of gall." So with men. If you would win a man to your cause, first convince him that you are his sincere friend. Therein is a drop of honey that catches his heart, which, say what he will, is the great highroad to his reason, and which, when once gained, you will find but little trouble in convincing his judgment of the justice of your cause, if indeed that cause really be a just one. On the contrary, assume to dictate to his judgment, or to command his action, or to mark him as one to be shunned and despised, and he will retreat within himself, close all the avenues to his head and his heart; and though your cause be naked truth itself, transformed to the heaviest lance, harder than steel, and sharper than steel can be made, and though you throw it with more than Herculean force and precision, you shall be no more able to pierce him than to penetrate the hard shell of a tortoise with a rye straw. Such is man, and so must he be understood by those who would lead him, even to his own best interests.

Practical philanthropists glow with a generous and brotherly zeal that mere theorizers are incapable of feeling. Benevolence and charity possess their hearts entirely; and out of the abundance of their hearts their tongues give utterance; "Love through all their actions runs, and all their words are mild." In this spirit they speak and act, and in the same they are heard and regarded. And when such is the temper of the advocate, and such of the audience, no good cause can be unsuccessful. But I have said that denunciations against dram-sellers and dram-drinkers are unjust, as well as impolitic. Let us see. I have not inquired at what period of time the use of intoxicating liquors commenced; nor is it important to know. It is sufficient that to all of us who now inhabit the world, the practice of drinking them is just as old as the world itself—that is, we have seen the one just as long as we have seen the other. When all such of us as have now reached the years of maturity first opened our eyes upon the stage of existence, we found intoxicating liquor recognized by everybody, used by everybody, repudiated by nobody. It commonly entered into the first draught of the infant and the last draught of the dying man. From the sideboard of the parson down to the ragged pocket of the houseless loafer, it was constantly found. Physicians prescribed it in this, that, and the other disease; government provided it for soldiers and sailors; and to have a rolling or raising, a husking or "hoedown", anywhere about without it was positively insufferable. So, too, it was everywhere a respectable article of manufacture and merchandise. The making of it was regarded as an honorable livelihood, and he who could make most was the most enterprising and respectable. Large and small manufactories of it were everywhere erected, in which all the earthly goods of their owners were invested. Wagons drew it from town to town; boats bore it from clime to clime, and the winds wafted it from nation to nation; and merchants bought and sold it, by wholesale and retail, with precisely the same feelings on the part of the seller, buyer, and bystander as are felt at the selling and buying of plows, beef, bacon, or any other of the real necessaries of life. Universal public opinion not only tolerated but recognized and adopted its use.

III.

It is true that even then it was known and acknowledged that many were greatly injured by it; but none seemed to think the injury arose from the use of a bad thing, but from the abuse of a very good thing. The victims of it were to be pitied and compassionated, just as are the heirs of consumption and other hereditary diseases. Their failing was treated as a misfortune, and not as a crime, or even as a disgrace. If, then, what I have been saying is true, is it wonderful that some should think and act now as all thought and acted twenty years ago? And is it just to assail, condemn, or despise them for doing so? The universal sense of mankind on any subject is an argument, or at least an influence, not easily overcome. The success of the argument in favor of the existence of an overruling Providence mainly depends upon that sense; and men ought not in justice to be denounced for yielding to it in any case, or giving it up slowly, especially when they are backed by interest, fixed habits, or burning appetites.

What an ignorance of human nature does it exhibit, to ask or expect a whole community to rise up and labor for the temporal happiness of others, after themselves shall be consigned to the dust, a majority of which community take no pains whatever to secure their own eternal welfare at no more distant day? Great distance in either time or space has wonderful power to lull and render quiescent the human mind. Pleasures to be enjoyed, or pains to be endured, after we shall be dead and gone are but little regarded even in our own cases, and much less in the cases of others.

But it is said by some that men will think and act for themselves; that none will disuse spirits or anything else because his neighbors do; and that moral influence is not that powerful engine contended for. Let us examine this. Let me ask the man who could maintain this position most stiffly, what compensation he will accept to go to church some Sunday and sit during the sermon with his wife's bonnet upon his head? Not a trifle, I'll venture. And why not? There would be nothing irreligious in it, nothing immoral, nothing uncomfortable — then why not? Is it not because there would be something egregiously unfashionable in it? Then it is the influence of fashion; and what is the influence of fashion but the influence that other people's actions have on our actions—the strong inclination each of us feels to do as we see all our neighbors do? Nor is the influence of fashion confined to any particular thing or class of things; it is just as strong on one subject as another. Let us make it as unfashionable to withhold our names from the temperance cause as for husbands to wear their wives' bonnets to church, and instances will be just as rare in the one case as the other.

"But," say some, "we are no drunkards, and we shall not acknowledge ourselves such by joining a reformed drunkards' society, whatever our influence might be." Surely no Christian will adhere to this objection. If they believe as they profess, that Omnipotence condescended to take on himself the form of sinful man, and as such to die an ignominious death for their sakes, surely they will not refuse submission to the infinitely lesser condescension, for the temporal, and perhaps eternal, salvation of a large, erring, and unfortunate class of their fellow-creatures. Nor is the condescension very great. In my judgment such of us as have never fallen victims have been spared more by the absence of appetite than from any mental or moral superiority over those who have. Indeed, I believe if we take habitual drunkards as a class, their heads and their hearts will bear an advantageous comparison with those of any other class. There seems ever to have been a proneness in the brilliant and warm-blooded to fall into this vice— the demon of intemperance ever seems to have delighted in sucking the blood of genius and of generosity. What one of us but can call to mind some relative, more promising in youth than all his fellows, who has fallen a sacrifice to his rapacity? Shall he now be arrested in his desolating career? In that arrest all can give aid that will; and who shall be excused that can and will not? Far around as human breath has ever blown he keeps our fathers, our brothers, our sons, and our friends prostrate in the chains of moral death.

Assignment
1. Read the source text. Following the note outline model provided below, create a note outline for another three paragraphs. Choose the most important or interesting portions from Mr. Lincoln's speech.
2. From your outline, write a 3-paragraph composition. Each paragraph should follow the topic/clincher rule; the first sentence (topic) and the last sentence (clincher) should repeat or reflect two to three key words. Indicate by using a highlighter or making bold the key words which are repeated or reflected in the topic and clincher sentences.

Note Outline and Paragraph Models
The paragraph model provided below shows what your first draft might look like after you edit it for structure and style. It contains the six dress-ups and all of the sentence openers. Note that key words in bold in the last (clincher) sentence repeat key words from the first (topic) sentence. By doing this, you make your paragraphs more unified.

Abraham on Temperance in the 1800's

I. testimonials, changed lives
   1. movement growing, rejoice
   2. preachers, lawyers, hired agents
   3. real testimony, reformed
   4. tears, joy, fed, clothed,
   5. too much denunciation, driven (push), doesn't work
Clincher: repeat (or reflect) 2-3 keywords from the topic.
	❺While we study the temperance movement, it should be remembered that without **changing lives**, it would have **meant** nothing. ❶We should try to understand the sources for growth and joyous success, <u>which</u> allow us to foretell the future. ❷With preachers, lawyers, and hired agents too much pushing may occur, but the truly powerful pull comes from the <u>enduring and everlasting</u> testimony of the reformed. ❻They are saved. ❸Joyously, their children are fed and <u>warmly</u> clothed again. ❸Miraculously, their wives are <u>deeply</u> cherished and nurtured again. ❹Appearing the saviors, preachers, lawyers and others may <u>command and move</u> them, but too much pushing doesn't work <u>because</u> the real success takes **meaning** only in the form of **changed lives**.

Note Outline: Abraham Speaks on Temperance
On a separate sheet of paper, together with your teacher, create your note outline for summarizing the rest of the speech in two paragraphs.

55

Style Tools and Examples
Sentence Openers, Part 2 (Level B & C now, Level A later)

Here are the remaining sentence openers you were wondering about when you read the paragraph model on the previous page:

❹ **"-ing"/"-ed" openers:** This type of sentence always requires a comma. The subject, which begins with a noun/pronoun/article, comes directly after the comma. In the following examples, the subject is italicized.

> **Appearing** over the horizon, *the soldier* limped wearily away.
> **Seated** for a moment, *he* sought to rest.

❺ **Adverb clausal opener:** Previously you used an adverb clause in the middle or end of a sentence. You can also begin a sentence with an adverb clause. Note again that a comma is always necessary, and the subject follows it directly.

> **When** he ran away, the army considered him AWOL.
> **While** he wined, dined and caroused, his money slipped away.

❻ **A VSS** is a very short sentence of five words or less (not a fragment). Writing can often be long, rambling, and monotonous. Use a VSS in every paragraph to grab the reader's attention.

> The army left one soldier with savings of $10,000. **He invested it.**
> He sat quietly before the jury. **The judge raised his gavel.**
> **They are saved.**

Practice: Rewrite the #1 sentence as a #4 ("-ing") and as a #5 (clausal) opener:

❶ We will someday see God face to face and understand His mysteries.

❹ *Seeing God face-to-face,* _____.

❺ *When we go to be with the Lord,* _____.

Practice: Now rewrite the #1 sentence in all six opener patterns:

❶ Those who have love do not take pleasure in evil, but rejoice in truth.

❷ _____

_____.

❸ _____

❹ _____.

_____

_____.

❺ _____

_____.

❻ _____

_____.

Checksheet for Lesson 10

Levels A, B, & C

Presentation
___ title centered and underlined
___ name, date
___ clearly presented

Mechanics
___ indent paragraphs
___ complete sentences
___ capitals (uppercase)
___ punctuation

Structure
___ follows model
___ paragraphs roughly equal size
___ topic and clincher sentences
     repeat or reflect 2-3 key words

Style Tools
___ underline dress-ups (one of each)
___ no "banned" adjectives
___ no "banned" verbs

Sentence Openers (B & C only)
___ ❶ subject
___ ❷ preposition
___ ❸ "-ly" word
___ ❹ "ing"/"ed" opener
___ ❺ adverb clausal opener
___ ❻ VSS (<5 words)

Paragraphs   I.   II.   III.

Level A

Dress-Ups
"-ly" word ___ ___ ___
"who/which" clause ___ ___ ___
"because" clause ___ ___ ___
quality adjective
adverb clause
(www.asia) ___ ___ ___
 strong verb ___ ___ ___

Level B

Dress-Ups
"-ly" word ___ ___ ___
"who/which" clause
(no "to be" verbs with
"who/which") ___ ___ ___
"because" clause ___ ___ ___
quality adjective ___ ___ ___
adverbial clause
(www.asia) ___ ___ ___
strong verb ___ ___ ___
sentence openers
  (#1, #2, #3, #5) ___ ___ ___

Level C

Dress-Ups
dual "-ly" word ___ ___ ___
"who/which" clause ___ ___ ___
invisible "who/which"
(no "to be" verbs with
"who/which") ___ ___ ___
dual adjectives ___ ___ ___
adverbial clause ___ ___ ___
strong verbs ___ ___ ___
sentence openers ___ ___ ___

Lesson 11: The Faith of St. Francis

Objective
To learn to create outlines by topic, in this case, three paragraphs on one theme – faith.

Source Text

On a certain morning in 1208, Francis was hearing Mass in the chapel of St. Mary of the Angels, near which he had then built himself a hut; the Gospel of the day told how the disciples of Christ were to possess neither gold nor silver, nor scrip for their journey, nor two coats, nor shoes, nor a staff, and that they were to exhort sinners to repentance and announce the Kingdom of God. Francis took these words as if spoken directly to himself, and so as soon as Mass was over he threw away the poor fragment left him of the world's goods, his shoes, cloak, pilgrim staff, and empty wallet. At last he had found his vocation. Having obtained a coarse woolen tunic of "beast color", the dress then worn by the poorest Umbrian peasants, and tied it round him with a knotted rope, Francis went forth at once exhorting the people of the countryside to penance, brotherly love, and peace.	Yet strong and definite as the saint's faith convictions were, he was never a slave to a theory in regard to the observances of poverty or anything else; about him indeed, there was nothing narrow or fanatical. As for his attitude towards study, Francis desiderated for his friars only such theological knowledge as was conformable to the mission of the order, which was before all else a mission of example. Hence he regarded the accumulation of books as being at variance with the poverty his friars professed. Francis resisted the eager desire for mere book learning, so prevalent in his time. This prevalent desire of his time struck at the roots of his simplicity and threatened to stifle the spirit of prayer, which Francis accounted preferable to all else.	Francis devoted himself to evangelizing Central Italy in 1213. About this time he received from Count Orlando of Chiusi the mountain of La Verna, an isolated peak among the Tuscan Apennines, rising some 4000 feet above the valley of the Casentino, as a retreat, "especially favorable for contemplation", to which he might retire from time to time for prayer and rest. For, in his faith walk, Francis never altogether separated the contemplative from the active life, as the several hermitages associated with his memory, and the quaint regulations he wrote for those living in them bear witness. At one time, indeed, a strong desire to give himself wholly to a life of contemplation seems to have possessed the saint.

Assignment

1. Read the three columns on the previous page, then create a note outline using the space provided. Choose key words from the most interesting or important facts, considering which ones will help you most build on the theme of faith.
2. From your outline, write a three-paragraph composition on these three remarkable examples of faith. Be sure to follow the checksheet on page 63. Also, remember to follow the topic-clincher rule and to highlight (or make bold) the key words which are reflecting or repeating.
3. As usual, edit carefully, get a second opinion, and rewrite or type a final draft. Be sure to save your completed composition for use with a later assignment in Unit VIII.

Note Outline: The Faith of St. Francis

I. <u>Gospel Message, faith in action</u>

1. _____
2. _____
3. _____
4. _____
5. _____

Clincher

II. <u>Learning, faith, not fanatical</u>

1. _____
2. _____
3. _____
4. _____
5. _____

Clincher

III. <u>Faith, retreat, contemplation</u>

1. _____

2. _____

3. _____

4. _____

5. _____

Clincher

Style Tools and Examples
Strengthening Weak Verbs

As main verbs, forms of *to be* such as *is, are, was,* and *were* weaken your sentences. To avoid *to be* verbs, you can often do one or more of the following: (A) change the verb entirely, (B) change the verb ending, or (C) form a helping verb without a "to be" verb.

(Model) Francis was ready and willing.
    (A) Francis **experienced** tremendous willingness.
    (B) Francis **willed** his life to follow the gospel.
    (C) Francis **had been willing** for years.

Practice rewriting *to be* verbs by replacing the verbs in the following sentences using each of the ways discussed above.

1. Francis **was** never a slave to any theory.

    (A) _____

    (B) _____

    (C) _____

2. The Friars **were** worried because of their hunger.

    (A) _____

    (B) _____

    (C) _____

Sentence Openers (new for Level A, review for Levels B & C) **[Refer to preposition list on page 45.]** Following the examples, rewrite the sentences to include sentence openers #2 and #3.

(Subject)   ❶ **The people** saw Francis preaching to the birds.

(Preposition)   ❷ **From** the comfort of their homes, the people saw Francis preaching to the birds.

("-ly" word)   ❸ **Unexpectedly**, the people saw Francis preaching to the birds.

(Subject)   ❶ Francis did not separate the contemplative from the active.

(Preposition)   ❷ _____

("-ly" word)   ❸ _____

(Subject)   ❶ Count Orlando reached out to assist Francis in prayer.

(Preposition)   ❷ _____

("-ly" word)   ❸ _____

Style Note, Level A
In this assignment, write paragraphs with at least subject, prepositional, and "-ly" openers. Practice until you feel comfortable with these three. When you are confident, add the remaining openers one at a time as guided by your teacher.

Checksheet for Lesson 11

Levels A, B, & C

Presentation
___ title centered and underlined
___ name, date
___ clearly presented

Mechanics
___ indent paragraphs
___ complete sentences
___ capitals (uppercase)
___ punctuation

Structure
___ follows model
___ paragraphs roughly equal size
___ topic and clincher sentences repeat or reflect 2-3 key words
___ title reflects key words of final sentence in last paragraph

Style Tools
___ underline dress-ups (one of each)
___ no "banned" adjectives
___ no "banned" verbs

Sentence Openers (as required)
___ ❶ subject
___ ❷ preposition
___ ❸ "-ly" word
___ ❹ "ing"/"ed" opener
___ ❺ adverb clausal opener
___ ❻ VSS (<5 words)

Paragraphs	I.	II.	III.
Level A			
Dress-Ups			
"-ly" word	___	___	___
"who/which" clause	___	___	___
"because" clause	___	___	___
quality adjective	___	___	___
adverb clause (www.asia)	___	___	___
strong verb	___	___	___
Sentence Openers (#1, #2, #3)	___	___	___
Level B			
Dress-Ups			
"-ly" word	___	___	___
"who/which" clause (no "to be" verbs with "who/which")	___	___	___
quality adjective	___	___	___
adverbial clause (www.asia)	___	___	___
strong verb	___	___	___
Sentence Openers (#1, #2, #3, #5, #6)	___	___	___
Level C			
Dress-Ups			
dual "-ly" word	___	___	___
"who/which" clause	___	___	___
invisible "who/which" (no "to be" verbs with "who/which")	___	___	___
dual adjectives	___	___	___
adverbial clause	___	___	___
dual verbs	___	___	___
Sentence Openers (all)	___	___	___

Stylistic Decorations (Level C)

From now on, include one stylistic decoration in every paragraph. Use them moderately; try not to reuse decorations in a composition. The six decorations are:

1. Question
2. Conversation (quotations)
3. Simile and Metaphor
4. 3sss (three short staccato sentences)
5. Alliteration
6. Dramatic paragraph opening and closing

Question

In compositions, questions immediately get your audience to start wondering what their answers would be, interesting them in what you have to say. Suppose you are writing a composition about guns and gun control. You could effectively grab your reader's attention by writing,

"Should handguns be controlled, licensed, registered or even banned?"

Or, if you were writing a composition about the importance of knowing a second language, you might begin with the following question,

"In many countries, students are required to learn English as they study their native language. In addition, most of the world recognizes English as the primary international language. Given these facts, why do so many Americans still seek to learn a foreign language"?

Conversation (Quotations)

In a narrative composition, (for example, "The Fox and the Crow") you *could* tell the story without conversation, but a few lines of dialogue would add variety.

The fox sat down and smirked. Putting on his most debonair air, he began, "My dear crow, most gorgeous creature in the woods, I swoon when you sing. Will you please favor me with a tune?"

Quotations also have a place in creative writing. The passage below, taken from Keats' "Ode to a Nightingale", is one of the most profound expressions of loneliness in a strange place.

"Perhaps the self same song that found a path
Through the sad heart of Ruth, when, sick for home,
She stood in tears amid the alien corn."

You can work passages such as this into your own writing. For example,

> *"There I was in the heart of the city – alone, fearful, and hungry. Lost in the traffic I felt like Ruth, homesick, standing 'in tears among the alien corn.' How terribly alien this new city seemed to me."*

You can also use quotations to add to history reports, biographical accounts, and various other assignments.

> *In a letter dated 1859, President Lincoln entreated, "Those who deny freedom to others, deserve it not for themselves; and, under a just God, can not long retain it."*

Similes and Metaphors
Similes and metaphors draw comparisons between two seemingly unlike or unrelated things. A simile uses "like" or "as", where a metaphor does not.

> *The wind was a torrent of darkness among the gusty trees,*
> *The moon was a ghostly galleon tossed upon cloudy seas,*
> *The road was a ribbon of moonlight over the purple moor.*

In this passage from Alfred Noyes, the wind was not a torrent, the moon was not a galleon (a type of ship), and the road was not a ribbon. They are all metaphors, which could have been converted to similes by adding the word "like" to each line. For instance, "The moon was like a ghostly galleon…"

Try to use metaphors and similes in your writing on a regular basis. In compositions longer than 5 paragraphs, for example, you could write a simile into one paragraph and a metaphor into another.

Three Short Staccato Sentences (3sss)
Three short sentences provide emphasis and attract the reader's attention, especially if they follow certain patterns, such as 4:4:4 (4 words in each sentence) or 4:3:2 (each sentence has one word less than the one before it).

> *Bulls approach me. They surround me. They encompass me. [3:3:3:]*

Using 3sss also gives you the opportunity to use an occasional sentence fragment for extra emphasis. Be careful, though; while sentence fragments can be effective, they can also confuse your reader if you overuse them.

Alliteration
Alliteration is the repetition of initial sounds in adjacent words or syllables. Examples of alliteration:

> *Dust of death   Down to the dust   Ravening and roaring lion (This one is a double alliteration: two sounds repeat, the "r" and the "ing" sounds.)*

Dramatic Paragraph Openings and Closings
The dramatic paragraph opening and closing requires that the topic sentence of the paragraph always comes first in the paragraph – except when you have a dramatic opening of five words or less. The dramatic opening, a VSS, comes just before the topic sentence. The dramatic closing is the last sentence of the paragraph. If your composition is short (up to five paragraphs), when you write in a dramatic opening, you must end with a dramatic closing. Later, in larger compositions, you can use a dramatic opening or closing alone in the paragraph.

"Here I am, Lord." Faithfully, Francis answered God's call and solemnly set out with his Friars toward Rome.
(Paragraph Details Here)
Answering God's call, Francis faithfully and humbly led his followers to serve the poor. Francis served the Lord.

Unit V: Writing Stories From Pictures
Lesson 12: The Sixteenth President of the United States

Objective
To learn to obtain details, factual or imagined, from a set of pictures.

Source Text

"I was born Feb. 12, 1809, in Hardin County, Kentucky. My parents were both born in Virginia, of undistinguished families—second families, perhaps I should say. My mother, who died in my tenth year, was of a family of the name of Hanks.... My father ... removed from Kentucky to ... Indiana, in my eighth year.... It was a wild region, with many bears and other wild animals still in the woods. There I grew up.... Of course when I came of age I did not know much. Still somehow, I could read, write, and cipher ... but that was all." Lincoln made extraordinary efforts to attain knowledge while working on a farm, splitting rails for fences, and keeping store at New Salem, Illinois.

He married Mary Todd, and they had four boys, only one of whom lived to maturity. In 1858 Lincoln ran against Stephen A. Douglas for Senator. He lost the election, but in debating with Douglas he gained a national reputation that won him the Republican nomination for President in 1860.

As President, he built the Republican Party into a strong national organization. Further, he rallied most of the northern Democrats to the Union cause. On January 1, 1863, he issued the Emancipation Proclamation that declared forever free those slaves within the Confederacy.

Lincoln never let the world forget that the Civil War involved an even larger issue. This he stated most movingly in dedicating the military cemetery at Gettysburg: "that we here highly resolve that these dead shall not have died in vain--that this nation, under God, shall have a new birth of freedom--and that government of the people, by the people, for the people, shall not perish from the earth."

Lincoln won re-election in 1864, as Union military triumphs heralded an end to the war. In his planning for peace, the President was flexible and generous, encouraging Southerners to lay down their arms and join speedily in reunion.

The spirit that guided him was clearly that of his Second Inaugural Address, now inscribed on one wall of the Lincoln Memorial in Washington, D. C. "With malice toward none; with charity for all; with firmness in the right, as God gives us to see the right, let us strive on to finish the work we are in; to bind up the nation's wounds.... " On Good Friday, April 14, 1865, Lincoln was assassinated at Ford's Theatre in Washington by John Wilkes Booth, an actor, who somehow thought he was helping the South. The opposite was the result, for with Lincoln's death, the possibility of peace with magnanimity died.

Assignment
1. Read the source text.
2. Read the Level A model composition that follows, noting style and structure elements. The Level A composition is short, less detailed than a Level B or C, and uses only three sentence openers. It follows the 3 pictures shown, one picture for each paragraph. The topic/clincher key words are in bold print.
3. As you read the model composition, fill in key words for the note outline. If you are a Level B or C student, prepare your own more detailed outline and composition appropriate to your level. Your first paragraph might begin something like this:

> *"Honest Abe, the pioneer son, worked hard growing up on the wild frontier of Kentucky, Indiana, and Illinois. Happily, he labored on a farm, split rails for fences, and kept store at New Salem, Illinois. Unfortunately, in New Salem he encountered a bully by the name of..." (Level C students might want to continue the paragraph drawing a simile between Abe's early fight and some later, seemingly unlike, and unrelated thing which somehow foreshadows his further struggles.)*

4. Place the sentence opener numbers in the margin, and underline the dress-ups. Highlight the key words in the topic and clincher sentences which repeat or reflect each other.

Structural Tools and Suggestions
Using a Picture's Central Fact
At all levels, the key introduction should be the topic sentence (the first in the paragraph). The clincher sentence (the last in the paragraph) should repeat or reflect 2-3 key words from the topic sentence.

The only element that must be mentioned is the central fact of the picture. Level B & C students will develop more facts and ideas beyond what is obviously seen in the picture.

Extracting Details from the Picture
Some people are better at seeing a picture and thinking of ways to describe it or things to say about it. One technique to help come up with the content is to ask yourself questions about the scene and the characters that may be portrayed. The answers to your questions then become the details for your outline. As you begin writing from your outline, more ideas will flow. Adding dress-ups and sentence openers will also help you to add detail. Some questions that may be helpful include:

Who is in the picture?
What are they   -doing?   -thinking?   -feeling?

Why is this situation happening?
When did this begin, or what happened just before this picture?
Where exactly is this, or what might be just outside this picture?
How is this being done, said?
What might happen after this picture?

Become a master at asking questions about pictures. The ability to ask oneself questions and hear answers is the core skill required for all creative writing and thinking. Practice asking questions constantly. Level B & C students will derive detail and further elaboration from simple pictures by asking these questions. Especially questions like, "What might be just outside this picture? What might happen right after this picture? What did happen just before this picture?"

Although the series of pictures might tell a story of sorts, it doesn't necessarily have to. Think of this model as "event description", where the topic sentence tells what's happening, and the rest of the paragraph explains what's going on in the minds of the participants and what's happening behind the scenes. It is a creative unit, so feel free to imagine what might have been, and have fun with it.

Style Tools and Examples
Synonyms
In compositions such as these, characters will be referred to many times, occasionally twice in one sentence. Rather than monotonously repeating the same words, find synonyms to use instead. Instead of writing "President Lincoln" over and over again, select these variations:
Abraham, the President, he, President Lincoln, honest Abe and the pioneer son.

President Lincoln: Note Outline   **Model Composition, Level A**

I. Central fact: Abe, fight

    1. _____

    2. _____

    3. _____

Clincher: Abe, fight

II. Central fact: speeches, inspired

    1. _____

    2. _____

    3. _____

    4. _____

Clincher: speeches, inspired

III. Central fact: visit, Lincoln Memorial

    1. _____

    2. _____

    3. _____

Clincher: visiting, Lincoln Memorial

When **Abe Lincoln** worked at the General Store in New Salem, Illinois, he got into a **fight** with the town bully. Unfortunately, that fight lasted a long time. But Abe and the town bully, Jack Armstrong, ended up becoming best friends. **Abe** and Jack would never **fight** again.

Abe delivered many **speeches** which **inspired** people. He studied to become a lawyer and a judge. He helped many people. Happily, he was able to represent the Republican Party and become the sixteenth President of the United States. He fought for the freedom of all people. **President Lincoln** had to **deliver** many **speeches** as he **inspired** the people and led them through the Civil War.

Today, we can **visit** the **Lincoln Memorial** in Washington, D.C. This monument honors a great man, Abraham Lincoln. Joyfully, I will travel to Washington D.C. with my family next summer. We will enjoy **visiting** the **Lincoln Memorial**.

Lesson 13: Mother Teresa in the Streets of Calcutta

Objective
To practice the skills demonstrated in Lesson 12. To read a story and rewrite it into a framework provided by three pictures. Remember the role of the central fact as it relates to the topic and clincher sentences in each paragraph.

Source Text

Once a chairman of a multinational corporation came to visit Mother Teresa. He was thinking of donating property to her cause. He asked her, "Mother, how do you manage your budget?" Mother Teresa replied by asking him who had sent him to her. He replied, "I felt an urge inside myself." Mother responded, "Other people like you come to see me and say the same thing. God has sent you as he sends each of the others who provide the material means we need for our work. The grace of God is what moved you. You are my budget."

Later, fourteen professors came from the United States from different universities. They had been to the home for the dying in Calcutta. Mother Teresa told them, "We have picked up more than 36,000 people only from the streets of Calcutta, and out of that big number more than 18,000 have died a beautiful death. They have just gone home to God." The professors discussed love and compassion with Mother, and then one of them asked, "Mother, please tell us something that we will remember." Mother Teresa replied, "Smile at each other, make time for each other in your family. Smile at each other." And then another professor asked, "Are you married?" Teresa said, "Yes, and I find it sometimes very difficult to smile at Jesus because he can be very demanding." She went on to say, "This is really something true, and there is where love comes—when it is demanding, and yet we can give it to Him with joy. We must live life beautifully, we have Jesus with us and He loves us. If we could only remember that God loves us, and we have an opportunity to love others as He loves us, not in big things, but in small things with great love."

The professors watched as Mother Teresa comforted a dying woman she had retrieved from a garbage dump. The woman's only lament was, "My son did this to me." Mother Teresa begged her, "You must forgive your son. In a moment of madness, when he was not himself, he did a thing he regrets. Be a mother to him—forgive him." Just before the woman died in the arms of Mother Teresa, she was able to express real forgiveness toward her son. She was not concerned that she was dying. It was the breaking of the heart that her son did not want her. Everyone present shared in this moment of suffering bringing dignity, compassion, love, understanding and real presence into the final moments of the dying woman's life. This exemplified the ministry of Mother Teresa – this ministry of presence, sharing in the pain and understanding.

Assignment
1. Read the source text. Study the three pictures on the following page and decide how the story can be formatted in three paragraphs matching the pictures. Make an outline in the space provided.
2. Write a three-paragraph composition on Mother Teresa. Double-space your first draft and, using your checksheet, proofread your composition to make sure you have all the elements required for your level.
3. Remember to highlight or bold print/type the key words in your topic and clincher sentences that repeat or reflect the main idea in the picture.
4. When you prepare your final composition, photocopy the pictures and paste them with the appropriate paragraph, as shown in the President Lincoln model. (Preferably, the pictures should go above or next to the paragraph.)

Style Tools and Examples
Punctuating Lists
Often, writers need to list several items in one sentence. It is important to use commas properly to avoid confusion. Structure your lists following the examples below.

Three items: Abe read Matthew, Mark, and Luke's Gospels.

Four items: Teresa built a house, gathered the dying, gathered food and medicine, and waited for the funds to rain in.

Five items: Francis developed a vocation based on humility, poverty, faith, service, and commitment.

Using Commas with Lists
There exists a difference of opinion in how commas should be used when listing similar items. Twentieth century American punctuation seems to lean toward using a comma after a second item in a list and before the conjunction, as in:

He ate apples, oranges, and pears.

This is generally referred to as the "Oxford" comma, or less commonly the "Harvard" comma, which came about because both Oxford University Press and Harvard University Press favor it. Technically, it is called the "serial" comma. The argument in favor of the second comma in a list of three things is that it often helps reduce ambiguity, which can be seen in statements such as this book dedication:

To my parents, Ayn Rand and God.

Ultimately, whether you should use the second comma or not depends on clarity, your publisher or your teacher, and your personal preference.

As you make your notes, remember to ask yourself questions about the pictures and the story:

Who is in the picture?
What are they doing?
  -thinking?
  -feeling?
How is this being done, said?
Why is this situation happening?

When did this begin, or what happened just before?
Where exactly is this, or what might be just outside this picture?
What might happen after this picture?

Outline: Mother Teresa in the Streets of Calcutta

    I.   Central fact:

        1. _____

        2. _____

        3. _____

        4. _____

        5. _____
Clincher

    II.   Central fact:

        1. _____

        2. _____

        3. _____

        4. _____

        5. _____
Clincher

    III.   Central fact:

        1. _____

        2. _____

        3. _____

        4. _____

        5. _____
Clincher

Checksheet for Lesson 13

Levels A, B, & C

Presentation
___ title centered and underlined
___ name, date
___ clearly presented

Mechanics
___ indent paragraphs
___ complete sentences
___ capitals (uppercase)
___ punctuation

Structure
___ follows model
___ paragraphs roughly equal size
___ topic and clincher sentences repeat or reflect 2-3 key words
___ title reflects key words of final sentence in last paragraph

Style Tools
___ underline dress-ups (one of each)
___ no "banned" adjectives
___ no "banned" verbs

Sentence Openers (as required)
___ ❶ subject
___ ❷ preposition
___ ❸ "-ly" word
___ ❹ "ing"/"ed" opener
___ ❺ adverb clausal opener
___ ❻ VSS (<5 words)

Paragraphs	I.	II.	III.
Level A			
Dress-Ups			
"-ly" word	___	___	___
"who/which" clause	___	___	___
"because" clause	___	___	___
quality adjective	___	___	___
adverb clause (www.asia)	___	___	___
strong verb	___	___	___
Sentence Openers (#1, #2, #3)	___	___	___
Level B			
Dress-Ups			
"-ly" word	___	___	___
"who/which" clause (no "to be" verbs with "who/which")	___	___	___
dual adjective	___	___	___
adverbial clause (www.asia)	___	___	___
strong verb	___	___	___
Sentence Openers (all)	___	___	___
Level C			
Dress-Ups			
dual "-ly" word	___	___	___
"who/which" clause	___	___	___
invisible "who/which" (no "to be" verbs with "who/which")	___	___	___
dual adjectives	___	___	___
adverbial clause	___	___	___
dual verbs	___	___	___
Sentence Openers (all)	___	___	___
Decoration (one/paragraph)	___	___	___

Lesson 14: The Character of St. Francis

Objective
To practice writing a composition within the framework provided by three pictures and a source text. Keep in mind the role of the central fact of each picture as it relates to the topic and the clincher in each paragraph.

Source Text

It has been said with pardonable warmth that Francis entered into glory in his lifetime, and that he is the one saint whom all succeeding generations have agreed in canonizing. Certain it is that those also who care little about the order he founded, and who have but scant sympathy with the Church to which he ever gave his devout allegiance, even those who know Christianity to be Divine, find themselves, instinctively as it were, looking across the ages for guidance to the wonderful "Umbrian Poverello". This unique position Francis doubtless owes in no small measure to his singularly lovable and winsome personality. There was about Francis, moreover, a chivalry and a poetry which gave to his other-worldliness a quite romantic charm and beauty. And this exquisite human element in Francis's character was the key to that far-reaching, all-embracing sympathy, which may be almost called his characteristic gift.

Heedless as Francis ever was of the world's judgments in his own regard, it was always his constant care to respect the opinions of all and to wound the feelings of none. Wherefore he admonishes the friars to use only low and mean tables, so that "if a beggar were to come to sit down near them he might believe that he was but with his equals and need not blush on account of his poverty." One night, we are told, the friary was aroused by the cry, "I am dying." "Who are you", exclaimed Francis arising, "and why are you dying?" "I am dying of hunger", answered the voice of one who had been too prone to fasting. Whereupon Francis had a table laid out and sat down beside the famished friar, and lest the latter might be ashamed to eat alone, ordered all the other brethren to join in the repast.

Above all it is his dealings with the erring that reveal the truly Christian spirit of his charity. Writing to a certain minister in the order, Francis says: "Should there be a brother anywhere in the world who has sinned, no matter how great so ever his fault may be, let him not go away after he has once seen thy face without showing pity towards him; and if he seek not mercy, ask him if he does not desire it. And by this I will know if you love God and me." Again, to medieval notions of justice the evildoer was beyond the law and there was no need to keep faith with him. But according to Francis, not only was justice due even to evildoers, but justice must be preceded by courtesy as by a herald. Courtesy, indeed, in the saint's quaint concept, was the younger sister of charity and one of the qualities of God Himself, Who "of His courtesy", he declares, "gives His sun and His rain to the just and the unjust." This habit of courtesy Francis ever sought to enjoin on his disciples. "Whoever may come to us," he writes, "whether a friend or a foe, a thief or a robber, let him be kindly received."

Hardly less engaging than his boundless sense of fellow feeling was Francis's downright sincerity and artless simplicity. "Dearly beloved," he once began a sermon following upon a severe illness, "I have to confess to God and you that during this Lent I have eaten cakes made with lard." And when the guardian insisted for the sake of warmth upon Francis having a fox skin sewn under his worn-out tunic, the saint consented only upon condition that another skin of the same size be sewn outside. For it was his singular study never to hide from men that which was known to God.

Another winning character trait of Francis which inspires the deepest affection was his unswerving directness of purpose and unfaltering following after an ideal. His dearest desire so long as he lived was ever to seek among wise and simple, perfect and imperfect, the means to walk in the way of truth. To Francis love was the truest of all truths; hence his deep sense of personal responsibility towards his fellows. The love of Christ and Him Crucified permeated the whole life and character of Francis, and he placed the chief hope of redemption and redress for a suffering humanity in the literal imitation of his Divine Master. The saint imitated the example of Christ as literally as it was in him to do so; barefoot, and in absolute poverty, he proclaimed the reign of love. This heroic imitation of Christ's poverty was perhaps the distinctive mark of Francis's vocation, and he was undoubtedly the most ardent, enthusiastic, and desperate lover of poverty the world has yet seen. The duty of a servant of God, Francis declared, was to lift up the hearts of men and move them to spiritual gladness.

Francis bridged the chasm between an aristocratic clergy and the common people, and though he taught no new doctrine, he so extensively re-popularized the old one given on the Mount that the Gospel took on a new life and called forth a new love.

Assignment
1. Read the source text.
2. Carefully examine the series of pictures corresponding to this assignment. Determine key words to help you make a topic sentence for each paragraph which reflects the central fact of the picture. Ask questions of yourself to fill in the details, based on the picture, the source text, and your ideas about what might have been happening in this story. The pictures may represent just a portion of the source text.
3. Write a 3-paragraph composition on the story, correlating the pictures and the written account. Use the checklist, and be sure to underline dress-ups, and mark sentence openers with numbers in the margin (or in brackets if typed). Level C students should also include one decoration

in each paragraph, and put "dec" in the margin on the line where it occurs.

Style Tools and Examples
"-ing"/ "-ed" openers (New for Level A, Review for Levels B & C)
A sentence that begins with an "-ing" or "-ed" opener **must** have a comma directly before the subject. Study the examples below where sentences that begin with ordinary subject openers get transformed into stronger sentences with an "-ing" or "-ed" opener. Subjects are in italics and commas appear before them. By using an "-ing" or "-ed" opener, you can also avoid weak verbs that use *is, are, was,* and *were.* Remember, when you use sentence openers in your compositions, put the number "4" in the margin.

1. (Model) The boy was jogging along the road and spied a deer. ▶ **Jogging** along the road, *the boy* spied a deer.
2. (Model) Francis was praying to God and pet the hungry wolf. ▶ **Praying** to God, *Francis* pet the hungry wolf.
3. (Model) She was trembling with fear and approached Mother Teresa. ▶ **Trembling** with fear, *she* approached Mother Teresa.

Practice: Convert the following into an "-ing" or "-ed" opener, remembering the comma.
1. Teresa was thoughtful after the professor's visit and felt grateful to the Lord. ▶

   _____

2. Abe was traveling to Washington D.C. to represent his party. ▶

   _____

3. People were gathered around the wolf and watched in wonder. ▶

   _____

As you make your notes, remember to ask yourself questions about the pictures and the story:

Who is in the picture?
What are they doing?
    -thinking?
    -feeling?
How is this being done, said?
Why is this situation happening?

When did this begin, or what happened just before?
Where exactly is this, or what might be just outside this picture?
What might happen after this picture?

Outline: Francis

I. Central fact:

    1._____

    2._____

    3._____

    4._____

    5._____
Clincher

II. Central fact:

    1._____

    2._____

    3._____

    4._____

    5._____
Clincher

III. Central fact:

    1._____

    2._____

    3._____

    4._____

    5._____
Clincher

Checksheet for Lesson 14

Levels A, B, & C

Presentation
___ title centered and underlined
___ name, date
___ clearly presented

Mechanics
___ indent paragraphs
___ complete sentences
___ capitals (uppercase)
___ punctuation

Structure
___ follows model
___ paragraphs roughly equal size
___ topic and clincher sentences repeat or reflect 2-3 key words
___ title reflects key words of final sentence in last paragraph

Style Tools
___ underline dress-ups (one of each)
___ no "banned" adjectives
___ no "banned" verbs

Sentence Openers (as required)
___ ❶ subject
___ ❷ preposition
___ ❸ "-ly" word
___ ❹ "ing"/ "ed" opener
___ ❺ adverb clausal opener
___ ❻ VSS (<5 words)

Paragraphs	I.	II.	III.
Level A			
Dress-Ups			
"-ly" word	___	___	___
"who/which" clause	___	___	___
"because" clause	___	___	___
quality adjective			
adverb clause (www.asia)	___	___	___
strong verb	___	___	___
Sentence Openers (#1, #2, #3)	___	___	___
Level B			
Dress-Ups			
"-ly" word	___	___	___
"who/which" clause (no "to be" verbs with "who/which")	___	___	___
dual adjective	___	___	___
adverbial clause (www.asia)			
strong verb	___	___	___
Sentence Openers (all)	___	___	___
Level C			
Dress-Ups			
dual "-ly" word	___	___	___
"who/which" clause	___	___	___
invisible "who/which" (no "to be" verbs with "who/which")	___	___	___
dual adjectives			
adverbial clause	___	___	___
dual verbs	___	___	___
Sentence Openers (all)	___	___	___
Decoration (one/paragraph)	___	___	___

Unit VI: Research Reports
Lesson 15: Abraham and Austin Gollaher

Objective
To begin to understand the complexities of writing from multiple sources, and to introduce the fused outline.

Source Texts

Source 1	Source 2
Austin Gollaher once saved Abraham Lincoln's life. The two boys had been going to school together one year; but the next year there was no school, because there were so few scholars to attend, there being only about 20 in the school the year before. Consequently Abe and Austin had not much to do; but as they did not go to school and their mothers were strict with them, they did not get to see each other very often. One Sunday morning Austin's mother woke him up early, saying she was going to see Mrs. Lincoln, and that he could go along. Glad of the chance, Austin was soon dressed and ready to go. After the two arrived, Abe and Austin played all through the day. While the boys were wandering up and down a stream called "Knob Creek", Abe said: "Right up there"—pointing to the east—"we saw a covey of partridges yesterday. Let's go over and get some of them." The stream was swollen and was too wide for them to jump across. Finally, they saw a narrow foot-log, and concluded to try it. It was narrow, but Abe said, "Let's do it." Austin went first and reached the other side. Abe went about halfway across, when he got scared and began	In 1816, when Abraham was just seven years old, an incident occurred while he played with a boy by the name of Austin Gollaher. The two were great friends and often got into mischief together. Once, they played hooky from school and Abe almost drowned. Abe and Austin were inseparable. They spent almost every day together when school was over and their chores were done. One day, the two boys were wandering up and down "Knob Creek" which was a small little stream that barely had any water in it at all. On this particular day the stream was unusually swollen, and so they decided to cross on a log that had fallen across the waterway. Abe said, "Let's coon it." And the two began to crawl on all fours like raccoons across the foot-log. During the crossover the boys were horsing around and both fell into the stream. Austin stood and waded the rest of the way, but Abe got stuck with his face in the water. So, Austin poked him with a long stick which Abe immediately grabbed and clung on to. Austin quickly realized that Abe wasn't kidding around so he held fast and pulled Abe across the rest of the way. Some water poured out of Abe's mouth, and he was soon right as rain after a long cough.

trembling. Austin hollered to him, "Don't look down nor up nor sideways, but look right at me and hold on tight!" But he fell off into the creek, and, as the water was about seven or eight feet deep, and neither boy could swim, Austin knew it would do no good for him to jump in after Abe.

So Austin got a stick—a long water sprout—and held it out to Abe. He came up, grabbed with both hands, and Austin put the stick into his hands. Abe clung to it, and Austin pulled him out on the bank, almost dead. Austin reported, "I got him by the arms and shook him well, and then rolled him on the ground, when the water poured out of his mouth."

He was alright very soon. The two boys promised never to tell anybody about the incident, and neither did for years. Austin told the story only after President Lincoln was assassinated.

The two boys decided to never tell about the incident, since they were supposed to be in school at the time and they didn't want a spanking. Austin lived to the ripe old age of 90 and recounted many stories like this one after the untimely passing of President Lincoln.

Assignment

1. Read each source, noting that there appears to be some factual and interpretational differences between them. How is a researcher to deal with interpretational differences?
2. You, the researcher, must weigh the evidence and determine what to present to your audience. It is important to develop your abilities of discernment and skill in handling discrepancies.
3. Study the outlines below. Notes were taken from source one; additional notes from source two. Some of the facts were the same or similar; some appear in one source but not the other. The chart on the right shows which details were used in the "fused" outline. Creating a chart such as this may be helpful for you as you take the notes and create the fused outline in the next two lessons.
4. Write a three paragraph composition using the fused outline provided, or adjusting it to your preferences. Follow the checksheet on page 89. As always, create your first draft, edit and rewrite or type a final copy.

Style Tools and Suggestions (all levels)

Similar to previous lessons, you may need to elaborate on the events, including details that are not explicitly stated in the source texts. You may not, however, feel comfortable if you think you are "adding facts". In this case where you need to make a supposition or assumption about what someone thought or said, you may find that "-ly" words such as "possibly," "probably," presumably," and "likely" would allow you some freedom to infer and describe details without changing or adding anything. In Units IV and VI, we are not really "telling a story" like we did in Units III and V; we are telling about – or reporting on -- events and facts. Therefore, we can use objective expressions like these to add detail without claiming any authority to know what is not directly written.

"One might imagine how…"   "We could suppose that…"

Notes and Fused Outline Models: Abraham and Austin Gollaher

The fused outline incorporates details from the note outlines you make from your sources. First, create note outlines for each paragraph of your sources. Then, review your outlines and choose details that you want to include in your report. In your fused outline, keep the number of details equal throughout your topics.

Note Outline: Source 1	Fused Outline	From Source 1	From Source 2
Austin Saves Abe			
- No school that year	I. Austin and Abe, best friends	√	√
- Mothers strict, not much time together	1. Boys play, Knob Creek		
- Rare Sunday Social Visit	2. Partridges seen, yesterday	√	
- Boys play, Knob Creek	3. Foot-log, creek deep	√	
- Partridges, Foot-log, Abe said, "Let's do it"	4. Abe- "Let's coon it", act like raccoons.		√
- Austin first, Abe halfway, terrified	Clincher		
- Abe fell, water deep, boys can't swim	II. Abe, slips and falls	√	
- Water sprout, Austin held it out	Boys can't swim	√	√
- Abe clung, Austin pulled	Abe under, Austin finds stick		
- Almost dead, rolled him, water poured out	Abe grabs, Austin pulls	√	√
- Quickly okay, boys not to tell anyone	Abe full of water, Austin rolls	√	
Note Outline: Source 2	Clincher		
- Mischief, hooky	III. Abe's okay		
- Every day together	Boys shaken	√	√
- "Let's coon it"	Oath to never tell		
- Both fell, Austin waded, Abe face-down	Austin broke, after Abe dead	√	√
- Afraid to tell, spanking	Austin lived to 90		
- Austin lived to 90, lots of stories	Clincher	√	√

Research Tools and Suggestions

Research, at its simplest, is the combination of two sources to create a third; this involves gathering materials such as facts, figures, and opinions from many sources to create a new theory or interpretation. A source is any place where you obtain information (i.e., books, magazines, videos, newspapers, and the Internet). As you practice research, you will learn to fuse multiple interpretations to draw a larger truth or to point out the differences between your sources.

Style Tools and Examples
Level C: Adjectival Teeter-totters

To make an adjectival "teeter-totter", place the dual adjectives dress-up just before the noun and the who/which clause after it. The noun forms the fulcrum of the teeter-totter. When you include this technique in your composition, the adjectives and who/which it uses will count as the minimum dress-up for the checklist.

1. (Model) The <u>weary old</u> **hunter** <u>who</u> climbed the hill sat a moment to rest.
   ∧

2. (Model) His <u>young and trusting</u> **son** <u>who</u> carried the gun stood by.
   ∧

Practice:

3. The _____(and/but/,) _____ **pair** <u>who</u>
   ∧
   _____, had faith in God.

4. God gave Abraham a _____ (and/but/,) _____ **test**
   ∧
   <u>which</u> _____.

5. Suddenly there arose a _____(and/but/,) _____
   wind <u>which</u> _____.
   ∧

Checksheet for Lessons 15 & 16

Levels A, B, & C

Presentation
___ title centered and underlined
___ name, date
___ clearly presented

Mechanics
___ indent paragraphs
___ complete sentences
___ capitals (uppercase)
___ punctuation

Structure
___ follows model
___ paragraphs roughly equal size
___ topic and clincher sentences repeat or reflect 2-3 key words
___ title reflects key words of final sentence in last paragraph

Style Tools
___ underline dress-ups (one of each)
___ sentence opener #'s marked
___ no "banned" adjectives
___ no "banned" verbs

Sentence Openers (as required)
___ ❶ subject
___ ❷ preposition
___ ❸ "-ly" word
___ ❹ "ing"/ "ed" opener
___ ❺ adverb clausal opener
___ ❻ VSS (<5 words)

Paragraphs	I.	II.	III.
Level A			
Dress-Ups			
"-ly" word	___	___	___
"who/which" clause	___	___	___
quality adjective	___	___	___
adverb clause (www.asia)	___	___	___
strong verb	___	___	___
Sentence Openers (#3, #4, #6)	___	___	___
Level B			
Dress-Ups			
"-ly" word	___	___	___
"who/which" clause	___	___	___
invisible "who/which"	___	___	___
dual adjective	___	___	___
adverbial clause (www.asia)	___	___	___
dual verbs	___	___	___
Sentence Openers (all)	___	___	___
Level C			
Dress-Ups			
dual "-ly" word	___	___	___
adjectival "teeter-totter"	___	___	___
invisible "who/which" (no "to be" verbs with "who/which")	___	___	___
adverbial clause	___	___	___
dual verbs	___	___	___
Sentence Openers (all)	___	___	___
Decoration (one/paragraph)	___	___	___

Lesson 16: Mother Teresa Receives for the Poor

Objective
To practice writing research reports from two or more sources. In this exercise there are three sources; you should try to use all of them.

Source Texts

"The other day I received 15 dollars from a man who has been on his back for twenty years, and the only part that he can move is his right hand. And the only companion that he enjoys is smoking. And he said to me: I do not smoke for one week, and I send you this money. It must have been a terrible sacrifice for him, but see how beautiful, how he shared, and with that money I bought bread and I gave to those who are hungry with a joy on both sides, he was giving and the poor were receiving. This is something that you and I can do - it is a gift of God to us to be able to share our love with others. And let it be as it was for Jesus. Let us love one another as he loved us. Let us love Him with undivided love. Let us keep that joy of loving Jesus in our hearts. And share that joy with all that we come in touch with. And that radiating joy is real, for we have no reason not to be happy. Christ is in our hearts, and Christ is in the poor that we meet so always smile even when it is difficult to smile". Nobel Lecture, 1979	Sacrificial giving is different than giving from our excess. Giving from our excess is like sharing some leftovers. Sacrificial giving comes from our core – we must sacrifice – giving up from our own immediate needs and wants. Sacrificial giving is always good for us. Sometimes it is obviously good for us – like the case of the man who gives up smoking and donates the money he would have spent on cigarettes to the poor. He may be saving his own health and his own life at the same time that he gives. Actually, we all save ourselves when we give sacrificially. Usually it doesn't involve giving up cigarettes, but always it involves giving up something. We can learn to see Christ in ourselves and in everyone we meet. Mother Teresa always saw Christ in everyone.	One man gave up smoking cigarettes so that he could donate the money instead to help feed the poor in Calcutta. He gave 15 dollars every week. Mother Teresa, or one of her helpers, would buy bread with those 15 dollars and distribute this food to the poor. The Sisters often felt like "middlemen" for God – acting as agents between those who give and those who receive. We can all give and share our love with others. It is a gift from God to be in a position of being able to give. Jesus gave himself completely for all of us. It is our duty to follow in the character of Jesus – to give what we can to assist our brothers and sisters. We must learn to see Christ in the poor that we meet. We can also see Christ in our own hearts, and in the smile that we give and the smile that we receive.

Assignment

1. Using the format taught in Lesson 15, take notes on each source so that you have 3 note outlines.
2. From your note outlines, create a fused outline. Place checkmarks (√) showing from which source each note came. Put the fused outline in the space provided. Remember that the report outline should have one Roman numeral and <u>not more than</u> five details for each paragraph.
3. Following your report outline, write a 3-paragraph report. Refer to the checksheet on page 89.
4. Review your first draft, adding any dress-ups and sentence openers you missed, and editing for improvements. Have it checked, then handwrite or type a final copy for your portfolio.

Note Outline

First Source: _____

1. _____
2. _____
3. _____
4. _____
5. _____

Second Source: _____

1. _____
2. _____
3. _____
4. _____

Third Source: _____

1. _____
2. _____
3. _____

Fused Outline

I. $15 Story

1. _____
2. _____
3. _____
4. _____
5. _____

Clincher

II. Sacrificial Giving

1. _____
2. _____
3. _____

Clincher

III. See Christ, poor

1. _____
2. _____
3. _____

Clincher

Lesson 17: Francis and the Wolf

Objective
To practice writing research reports from multiple sources, and adding in your own idea, opinion, perception or belief.

Source Texts

Once upon a time there was a wolf living near Gubbio, Italy so ravenous that it was not only killing and eating animals, but people, too. The people took up arms and went after it, but those who encountered the wolf perished. Villagers became afraid to leave the city walls.

Francis had pity on the people and decided to go out and meet the wolf. The people desperately warned him, but he insisted that God would take care of him.

Suddenly the wolf, jaws agape, charged out of the woods. Francis made the Sign of the Cross toward it. The power of God caused the wolf to slow down and to close its mouth.

Then Francis called out to the creature: "Come to me, Brother Wolf. In the name of Christ, I order you not to hurt anyone." At that moment the wolf lowered its head and lay down at St. Francis' feet, meek as a lamb.

St. Francis explained to the wolf that he had been terrorizing the people, killing not only animals, but humans who are made in the image of God. "Brother Wolf," said Francis, "I want to make peace between you and the people of Gubbio. They will harm you no more and you must no longer harm them. All past crimes are to be forgiven."

The wolf showed its assent by moving its body and nodding its head. Francis asked the wolf to make a pledge. As St. Francis extended his hand to receive the pledge, the wolf extended its front paw and placed it into the saint's hand. Then Francis commanded the wolf to follow him into town to make a peace pact with the townspeople. The wolf meekly followed St. Francis.

By the time they got to the town square, everyone was there to witness the miracle. With the wolf at his side, Francis gave the town a sermon on the wondrous and fearful love of God, calling them to repent from all their sins. Then he offered the townspeople peace, on behalf of the wolf. The townspeople promised in a loud voice to feed the wolf. Then Francis asked the wolf if he would live in peace under those terms. He bowed his head and twisted his body in a way that convinced everyone he accepted the pact. Then once again the wolf placed its paw in Francis' hand as a sign of the pact.

From that day on the people kept the pact they had made. The wolf lived for two years among the townspeople, going from door to door for food. It hurt no one and no one hurt it.

The Eskimo and the Indian understood that when the wolf is around, the herd of large animals such as deer and moose and caribou, will be strong. Without the wolf, these animals become weak and diseased. Wolves generally kill the weak, the old, and the young. If the wolf did not do this, the deer and the caribou and the moose and other large animals would damage the forest by overpopulating and eating the plants and trees.

The inherent nature of "civilized" man is to control that which he does not understand, otherwise destroy it. Man set out to destroy the wolf and nearly succeeded. As civilization rapidly progressed, people continued to distance themselves further from the wilderness, while the wolf remained a wild predator. People put up city walls and lived behind them.

Man is only just beginning to reach a simple knowledge of the wolf. The secrets remain hidden beneath a veil of misunderstanding. Man does not see the world of the wolf in its proper perspective and does not know how to come to terms with it. We tend to believe that we humans are the masters of creation and we refuse to accept that the animals are the ones who are constantly in touch with the realities by which we live and die on this planet.

The wolf can teach us. With its uncanny perceptions, and a social structure that closely resembles our own, wolves challenge us to be wise.

Did St. Francis understand something about animals that we could all benefit from? How did he communicate with them? Why did he have no fear? Did the animals recognize the living God working through the loving presence of St. Francis?

There is a legend about a sole wolf near Gubbio, Italy. It is very unusual for wolves to be found alone. They are highly social animals, they travel and hunt in packs. Was this really a wolf in Gubbio?

The public record shows that Francis tamed the animal and caused it to leave the people of Gubbio alone. In gratitude, the people of Gubbio fed the wolf, probably causing it to become spoiled and lazy, and to leave its pack. The animal died two years after its captivity in Gubbio.

Assignment

Your ultimate aim is to write a two-paragraph report on the miracle of the wolf using the two sources above and following the steps as outlined below.

1. As you read the two source texts, look for the two main topics available in the text (probably "the situation" and "the miracle").
2. Make two note outlines for each of the two topics, taking 3-5 details from each account. (If the lines provided here are not large enough, use extra blank paper.)
3. From the notes, create a two paragraph fused outline.
4. Following your fused outline, write up the report. Double-space your first draft.
5. Follow the topic/clincher rule and use the checklist provided to continue practice of your stylistic techniques.
6. Proofread your composition, following your checksheet, and get a second opinion.
7. Write or type your final draft, keeping it in your portfolio.

Structural Tools and Suggestions

In your second paragraph, which will likely focus on the miracle, you will certainly want to report the factual details, but you should also include a statement or two about the significance of this particular miracle. This would mean that you are specifically adding in your own idea, opinion, perception or belief. This is perfectly acceptable. Since your name is on the top of your paper under the title, the reader will see that this is your work, and there is no need to say in your report, "I think…", or "I believe that…" or "In my opinion…" Just say what you think, almost like it was another fact.

Qualifying your opinion with "I think…" and similar comments, is not only unnecessary, it weakens your writing. If you practice inserting one or two statements of commentary with your facts right now, essay writing (where you have to have an entire concluding paragraph with your own ideas and opinions) will be much easier.

Source Outlines, topic one

Situation:

1. _____

2. _____

3. _____

4. _____

5. _____

Situation:

1. _____

2. _____

3. _____

4. _____

5. _____

Source Outlines, topic two

Miracle:

1. _____
2. _____
3. _____
4. _____
5. _____

Miracle:

1. _____
2. _____
3. _____
4. _____
5. _____

Fused Outline, topic one

I. _____
1. _____
2. _____
3. _____
4. _____
5. _____

Clincher

Fused Outline, topic two

I. _____
1. _____
2. _____
3. _____
4. _____
5. _____

Clincher

Checksheet for Lesson 17

Levels A, B, & C

Presentation
___ title centered and underlined
___ name, date
___ clearly presented

Mechanics
___ indent paragraphs
___ complete sentences
___ capitals (uppercase)
___ punctuation

Structure
___ follows model
___ topic and clincher sentences repeat or reflect 2-3 key words
___ title reflects key words of final sentence in last paragraph

Style Tools
___ underline dress-ups (one of each)
___ sentence opener #'s marked
___ no "banned" adjectives
___ no "banned" verbs

Sentence Openers (as required)
___ ❶ subject
___ ❷ preposition
___ ❸ "-ly" word
___ ❹ "ing"/"ed" opener
___ ❺ adverb clausal opener
___ ❻ VSS (<5 words)

Paragraphs	I.	II.
Level A		
Dress-Ups		
"-ly" word	___	___
"who/which" clause	___	___
quality adjective	___	___
adverb clause (www.asia)	___	___
strong verb	___	___
Sentence Openers (#3, #4, #6)	___	___
Level B		
Dress-Ups		
dual "-ly" word	___	___
"who/which" clause	___	___
Invisible "who/which"	___	___
dual adjective	___	___
adverbial clause (www.asia)	___	___
dual verbs	___	___
Sentence Openers (all)	___	___
Level C		
Dress-Ups		
dual "-ly" word	___	___
adjectival "teeter-totter"	___	___
invisible "who/which" (no "to be" verbs with "who/which")	___	___
adverbial clause	___	___
dual verbs	___	___
Sentence Openers (all)	___	___
Decoration (one/paragraph)	___	___

Unit VII: Creative Writing
Lesson 18: The Civil War

Objective
To practice taking a topic and, using your imagination, creating a description or narrative.

When you contemplate creative descriptive writing, you must first think: what are some possible themes (topics)? For example, if someone asked you to write on a vacation you recently took, you might ask yourself what topics could possibly form your body paragraphs: 1) location, 2) who you were with, 3) traveling there, 4) food, and 5) what you did. Once you have a list of possible topics, you must choose three, for example: location, who, and what you did.

Then you could easily write a three-paragraph composition, the first paragraph with a topic and clincher using the "location" as a key word, the second paragraph talking about "who" vacationed with you, and the third paragraph explaining "what you did" on your vacation To make the composition more complete, you would then add in an introduction and a conclusion.

Structural Tools and Suggestions
Introductions
A good introduction offers some background on the topic mentioned in the title and suggests what the reader might expect to find in the composition. The introduction (or introductory paragraph) should:
1. be the same length as your other body paragraphs.
2. indicate time and place.
3. have one or two sentences of historical background to the subject.
4. state the three themes (topics).
5. end with the title.
6. conform to all the rules of style as in body paragraphs.
7. not have a topic or clincher sentence.

Conclusions
Conclusions should be one paragraph in length, approximately the same size as all the other paragraphs in the composition. In style they also conform to the body paragraphs. Just as in the introduction, they do not need topic sentences and it is good to end the introduction with key words from the title. Your conclusions should:
1. repeat the three themes (topics).
2. tell whet is most important and why.
3. tell which is least important and why.
4. end with the title.
5. never use "I" or "we".

Conclusions reveal the writer as no other paragraph does. What you decide is "most important" and why you decide it is most important reveal yourself as a writer. Sometimes, what you think is most important, someone else might feel is less important or even irrelevant. There is no right or wrong in creative writing; just be able to justify your choice.

Especially in descriptive creative writing, the key to good organization is "think three themes." Try to fit your ideas into three themes. We'll work on the body paragraphs later. From now on, give your composition an introductory paragraph, three body paragraphs, and a concluding paragraph.

Source Text

"I claim not to have controlled events, but confess plainly that events have controlled me." The Collected Works of Abraham Lincoln, edited by Roy P. Basler, Volume VII, "Letter to Albert G. Hodges" (April 4, 1864), p. 281.

"In giving freedom to the slave, we assure freedom to the free - honorable alike in what we give, and what we preserve. We shall nobly save, or meanly lose, the last best hope of earth. Other means may succeed; this could not fail. The way is plain, peaceful, generous, just - a way which, if followed, the world will forever applaud, and God must forever bless." Lincoln's Second Annual Message to Congress, December 1, 1862.

"With malice toward none, with charity for all, with firmness in the right as God gives us to see the right, let us strive on to finish the work we are in; to bind up the nation's wounds; to care for him who shall have borne the battle, and for his widow and his orphan - to do all which may achieve and cherish a just and lasting peace, among ourselves, and with all nations." Lincoln's Second Inaugural Address, March 4, 1865.

"A house divided against itself cannot stand. I believe this government cannot endure permanently half-slave and half-free. I do not expect the Union to be dissolved - I do not expect the house to fall - but I do expect it will cease to be divided. It will become all one thing or all the other." Lincoln's "House-Divided" Speech in Springfield, Illinois, June 16, 1858.

"Both parties deprecated war; but one of them would make war rather than let the nation survive; and the other would accept war rather than let it perish. And the war came." Lincoln's Second Inaugural Address, March 4,1865.

"I am rather inclined to silence, and whether that be wise or not, it is at least more unusual nowadays to find a man who can hold his tongue than to find one who cannot." The Collected Works of Abraham Lincoln, edited by Roy P. Basler, Volume IV, "Remarks at the Monogahela House" (February 14, 1861), p. 209.

"Fourscore and seven years ago our fathers brought forth on this continent a new nation, conceived in liberty and dedicated to the proposition that all men are created equal." Lincoln's Gettysburg Address on November 19,1863.

"Public sentiment is everything. With public sentiment, nothing can fail; without it nothing can succeed." <u>The Collected Works of Abraham Lincoln,</u> edited by Roy P. Basler, Volume III, "Lincoln-Douglas Debate at Ottawa" (August 21, 1858), p. 27.

"...that we here highly resolve that these dead shall not have died in vain; that this nation shall have a new birth of freedom; and that this government of the people, by the people, for the people, shall not perish from the earth." Lincoln's Gettysburg Address, November 19, 1863.

"I have never studied the art of paying compliments to women; but I must say that if all that has been said by orators and poets since the creation of the world in praise of women were applied to the women of America, it would not do them justice for their conduct during this war. I will close by saying, God bless the women of America!" <u>The Collected Works of Abraham Lincoln,</u> edited by Roy P. Basler, Volume VII, "Remarks at Closing of Sanitary Fair, Washington D.C." (March 18, 1864), p. 254.

"Whenever I hear any one arguing for slavery I feel a strong impulse to see it tried on him personally." <u>The Collected Works of Abraham Lincoln,</u> edited by Roy P. Basler, Volume VIII, "Speech to One Hundred Fortieth Indiana Regiment" (March 17, 1865), p. 361.

"The probability that we may fall in the struggle ought not to deter us from the support of a cause we believe to be just; it shall not deter me." <u>The Collected Works of Abraham Lincoln,</u> edited by Roy P. Basler, Volume I, "Speech on the Sub-Treasury" (in the Illinois House of Representatives, December 26, 1839), p. 178.

"Leave nothing for tomorrow which can be done today." <u>The Collected Works of Abraham Lincoln,</u> edited by Roy P. Basler, Volume II, "Notes for a Law Lecture" (July 1, 1850), p. 81.

"In regard to this Great Book [the Bible], I have but to say, it is the best gift God has given to man. All the good the Savior gave to the world was communicated through this book." <u>The Collected Works of Abraham Lincoln,</u> edited by Roy P. Basler, Volume VII, "Reply to Loyal Colored People of Baltimore upon Presentation of a Bible" (September 7, 1864), p. 542.

Assignment
1. Read the source text to get a feeling about the mind and character of President Lincoln during the time of the Civil War.

2. Read at least one book or article about the Civil War. You can also use the Internet to research the Civil War if you like. Decide what specific topics about the Civil War are most interesting to you. Focus your imagination on those topics – imagine yourself being there. If you like, you can imagine yourself being President Lincoln.

3. Write a 5-paragraph composition including an introduction and a conclusion on what you imagine the Civil War was like. Follow the creative writing procedure chart below. Be sure to include the style and structural elements for your level. Use the creative writing checksheet on page 101. Make an outline on a separate sheet of paper (following the model chart below) and then write the rough draft. Edit and type a final copy as always. This is creative writing, have fun!

Model Chart ▶ Because this unit requires you to "create" the ideas, you must get most of your ideas out of your brain. To do this, it is helpful to aggressively ask yourself questions: WHO? WHAT? WHERE? WHEN? WHY? HOW? BEST? WORST? PROBLEMS?	**I. Introduction** 1. Get attention of reader 2. Background (time, place) 3. State 3 themes (topics) **II. Topic** Details Clincher **III. Topic** Details Clincher **IV. Topic** Details Clincher **V. Conclusion** 1. Restate 3 themes (topics) 2. Most significant & why

Creative Writing Procedure for 5-Paragraph Descriptive Composition

Step 1: Determine subject.
Step 2: List possible topics.
Step 3: Choose 3 topics; determine order.
Step 4: Create outline and details. (Ask yourself questions)
Step 5: Write the body (topic) paragraphs.
Step 6: Write the introduction & conclusion paragraphs.

Checksheet for Lessons 18 & 19

Levels A, B, & C
 	
Presentation
___ title centered and underlined
___ name, date
___ clearly presented
 	
Mechanics
___ indent paragraphs
___ complete sentences
___ capitals (uppercase)
___ punctuation
 	
Structure
___ follows model
___ paragraphs roughly equal size
___ topic and clincher sentences
(BODY PARAGRAPHS ONLY)
___ repeat or reflect 2-3 key words
___ title reflects key words of final sentence in Conclusion **or** last sentence of Introduction
 	
Style Tools
___ underline dress-ups (one of each)
___ no "banned" adjectives
___ no "banned" verbs
 	
Sentence Openers
___ ❶ subject
___ ❷ preposition
___ ❸ "-ly" word
___ ❹ "ing"/ "ed" opener
___ ❺ adverb clausal opener
___ ❻ VSS (<5 words)
	Introduction **I.**
	  Time, place, historical background ___
	  Three themes (topics) ___
	  Ends with title ___
	  Stylistic techniques at your level ___
	
	Paragraphs **I.** **II.** **III.** **IV.** **V.**
	Level A
	
	  Dress-Ups
	    "-ly" word ___ ___ ___ ___ ___
	    "who/which" clause ___ ___ ___ ___ ___
	    quality adjective ___ ___ ___ ___ ___
	    adverb clause
	    (www.asia) ___ ___ ___ ___ ___
	    strong verb ___ ___ ___ ___ ___
	  Sentence Openers ___ ___ ___ ___ ___
	
	Level B
	
	  Dress-Ups
	    dual "-ly" words ___ ___ ___ ___ ___
	    "who/which" clause ___ ___ ___ ___ ___
	    invisible "who/which" ___ ___ ___ ___ ___
	    dual adjectives
	    adverbial clause
	    dual verb ___ ___ ___ ___ ___
	  Sentence Openers ___ ___ ___ ___ ___
	  Decoration ___ ___ ___ ___ ___
	
	Level C
	
	  Dress-Ups
	    dual "-ly" word ___ ___ ___ ___ ___
	    "who/which" clause ___ ___ ___ ___ ___
	    invisible "who/which" ___ ___ ___ ___ ___
	    adj. "teeter-totter" ___ ___ ___ ___ ___
	    adverbial clause
	    dual verbs
	  Sentence Openers ___ ___ ___ ___ ___
	  Decoration ___ ___ ___ ___ ___
	
	Conclusion **V.**
	  Repeats three themes (topics) ___
	  Most important? Why? ___
	  Least important? Why? ___
	  Stylistic techniques
	    (at your level) ___

Lesson 19: A Warning of the Assassination to Come

Objective
To practice creative writing as well as designing and writing introductions and conclusions.

Source Text

The Lincolns often stayed at The Lincoln Cottage located on the grounds of the Soldier's Home in Washington D.C. Abraham would ride his favorite horse from the White House to Soldier's Home.

One day in August 1864, a sniper apparently tried to assassinate President Lincoln. "About eleven o'clock that night, Private John W. Nichols of Company K was on guard duty at the large gate on the edge of the Soldier's Home grounds when he heard a rifle shot and then witnessed the "bareheaded" president riding quickly on horseback toward his cottage. Private Nichols asked the president about his missing hat and was told that "somebody had fired a gun off at the foot of the hill" which frightened Lincoln's horse and then led to a struggle to regain control that had "jerked his hat off." Concerned, Nichols recalled years later that he and another member of the company went down the twisting driveway toward the main road where they discovered the President's signature silk plug hat with a bullet hole through the crown. The next day Nichols claimed that he returned the item to the President, who assured him "rather unconcernedly" that the whole episode was the product of "some foolish gunner" and that he wanted the matter "kept quiet."

From that day on, Lincoln rode to and from the Soldiers' Home in a carriage, surrounded by soldiers. Whoever fired the shot remains a mystery to this day.

Assignment
Write a 5-paragraph creative composition with an introduction, 3-paragraph body and a conclusion describing the reaction people might have had resulting from either the first attempted assassination or the successful assassination of President Lincoln. While you will make up most of your composition, include facts given in the source text or found by your own research of the successful assassination. THINK of possible THEMES (topics).

While you can choose any three themes you wish, here are some ideas if you get stuck:
1. The reaction in an ordinary family home.
2. The reaction among the soldiers at Soldier's Home.
3. What the enemies' reaction might have been had Lincoln not had the strength of character to instruct that the matter be "kept quiet".

This composition is your creation. Use your imagination, but make sure you organize your ideas into three themes. Each one will take up an entire paragraph. Refer to the checksheet on page 101 to make sure you include all the style and structural elements required of your level.

Structural Tools and Suggestions
1. Review the Procedure Chart on page 100. It is usually best to write the three body paragraphs first and then write the introduction and conclusion based on what you have already written.
2. Be sure to include topic-clincher sentences in the body paragraphs, and to highlight (or bold) the topic key words in the introduction and conclusion as well.

Style Tools and Examples, (Levels B & C)
Triple "-ly" adverbs may be consecutive or spaced out, as in the following examples.

Consecutive
Abraham **strongly**, **repeatedly**, and **consistently** confronted the enemy.

Spaced
Left destitute by the thousands, many Civil War families **clearly** endured discrimination, **significantly** suffered a loss of wealth, and **ultimately** sacrificed their lives for a cause they believed in.

As a general rule, when putting three adverbs together, make sure they come from different categories on the accompanying chart. The three adverbs used in the first example above come from subsections I to III. Given its immense size, of course, three adverbs could easily be linked from subsection VI as in:

She walked beautifully, calmly and smoothly.
She walked calmly, smoothly yet anxiously.
She walked calmly, dreamily, but somewhat proudly.

The words *yet* and *but* help when putting together three which normally do not go together.

Adverbs: "-ly" Words				
I. Importance	II. Assurance	III. Frequency	IV. Sequence	V. Clincher Starters
entirely significantly substantially totally increasingly	assuredly presumably predictably fundamentally possibly	rapidly frequently continuously immediately easily	AVOID: firstly secondly thirdly	clearly assuredly frequently ultimately obviously

103

essentially consistently primarily customarily absolutely completely virtually seriously utterly distinctly notably	probably evidently undeniably readily normally clearly willingly surely regularly rigidly strictly successfully strongly understandable seriously	increasingly suddenly occasionally gently repeatedly quickly normally gradually constantly repeatedly steadily	CHOOSE: initially eventually ultimately originally effectively finally previously	undeniably gradually generally usually normally

VI. More Adverbs (can you think of additional ones?)

abnormally abruptly absentmindedly absolutely accusingly actually adversely amazingly angrily anxiously arrogantly assuredly awkwardly badly bashfully beautifully briskly calmly cheaply compassionately confidently crisply crossly daintily delicately determinedly doggedly dreamily	enormously enticingly entirely enviously especially essentially evidently exactly excitedly exclusively expertly extremely fairly famously fearlessly fervently foolishly freely frightfully gratefully greatly hatefully heavily impulsively intensely inwardly lawfully longingly	loudly madly marvelously meaningfully reluctantly reassuringly regretfully regularly righteously rigidly scarcely sedately seemingly sharply sheepishly sleepily slyly smoothly softly solidly speedily surprisingly suspiciously truly undeniably vastly vehemently vocally	willfully woefully yearningly zealously _____ _____ _____ _____ _____ _____ _____ _____ _____ _____ _____ _____ _____

Lesson 20: The Key Virtues of a Strong Character

Objective
To further practice creative writing, including an introduction and a conclusion, following the steps in the previous two lessons.

Assignment
1. Refer to the chart of *Key Virtues* listed on page 12 of this book. Select one of the three personalities of this book, either Mother Teresa, St. Francis or Abraham Lincoln, and then decide what top three virtues best describe that person.
2. Plan and write a 5-paragraph creative composition with an introduction, 3-paragraph body, and a conclusion.
3. The themes (topics) of your 3-paragraph body are each of the three key virtues you have selected.
4. Use the facts you have learned about Abraham Lincoln, Mother Teresa and/or St. Francis from the previous lessons of this book. You may also wish to do some additional reading on your selected personality. In addition, use your own imagination.
5. Remember to follow the process chart (below). Refer to the checksheet to make sure you include all the style and structural elements required of your level.

Step 1: Determine the subject.
Step 2: List possible topics. (in this case, from the chart on page 12)

_____   _____   _____
_____   _____   _____
_____   _____   _____

Step 3: Choose 3 topics; determine their order in the composition.
Step 4: Create an outline and details by taking "notes from your brain".
    Ask yourself questions about each topic.
Step 5: Write the body (topic) paragraphs.
Step 6: Write the introduction and conclusion paragraphs.

Style Tools and Examples
Accent, Level C
For the following words, if the accent is at the front of the word, it is a noun. If it is at the end, then it is a verb. Look at the word refuse. If the accent is *'ref-use*, it is a noun referring to garbage as in, "Put out the refuse since tomorrow is garbage day." When the accent comes at the end, *re-'fuse*, it is a verb, as in, "I refuse to do that." Study the following three examples and then write sentences in the blanks provided for practice.

1. (Model) 'en-trance: Where is the entrance to the White House?
   en-'trance: The bright new toys seemed to entrance the children.

2. (Model) 'pro-ceeds: They donated the proceeds from the banquet to Teresa.
   pro-'ceeds: After Francis leaves our home, he always proceeds to church.

3. (Model) 'con-fines: Please stay within the confines of the Soldier's Home.
   con-'fines: She confines the dog to the yard so he doesn't run off.

4. 'con-duct (n): _____
   con-'duct (v): _____

5. 'con-vict (n): _____
   con-'vict (v): _____

6. 'con-vert (n): _____
   con-'vert (v): _____

7. 'pres-ent (n): _____
   pres-'ent (v): _____

8. 'in-crease (n): _____
   in-'crease (v): _____

9. 'ob-ject (n): _____
   ob-'ject (v): _____

10. 'des-ert (n): _____
    de-'sert (v): _____

Checksheet for Lesson 20

Levels A, B, & C

Presentation
___ title centered and underlined
___ name, date
___ clearly presented

Mechanics
___ indent paragraphs
___ complete sentences
___ capitals (uppercase)
___ punctuation

Structure
___ follows model
___ paragraphs roughly equal size
___ topic and clincher sentences
(BODY PARAGRAPHS ONLY)
___ repeat or reflect 2-3 key words
___ title reflects key words of final sentence in Conclusion **or** last sentence of Introduction

Style Tools
___ underline dress-ups (one of each)
___ no "banned" adjectives
___ no "banned" verbs

Sentence Openers
___ ❶ subject
___ ❷ preposition
___ ❸ "-ly" word
___ ❹ "ing"/ "ed" opener
___ ❺ adverb clausal opener
___ ❻ VSS (<5 words)

Introduction	I.
Time, place, historical background	___
Three themes (topics)	___
Ends with title	___
Stylistic techniques at your level	___

Paragraphs	I.	II.	III.	IV.	V.
Level A					
Dress-Ups					
"-ly" word	___	___	___	___	___
"who/which" clause	___	___	___	___	___
quality adjective	___	___	___	___	___
adverb clause (www.asia)	___	___	___	___	___
strong verb	___	___	___	___	___
Sentence Openers	___	___	___	___	___

	I.	II.	III.	IV.	V.
Level B					
Dress-Ups					
dual "-ly" words	___	___	___	___	___
"who/which" clause	___	___	___	___	___
invisible "who/which"	___	___	___	___	___
dual adjectives	___	___	___	___	___
adverbial clause	___	___	___	___	___
dual verb	___	___	___	___	___
Sentence Openers	___	___	___	___	___
Decoration	___	___	___	___	___

	I.	II.	III.	IV.	V.
Level C					
Dress-Ups					
dual "-ly" word	___	___	___	___	___
"who/which" clause	___	___	___	___	___
invisible "who/which"	___	___	___	___	___
adj. "teeter-totter"	___	___	___	___	___
adverbial clause	___	___	___	___	___
dual verbs	___	___	___	___	___
Sentence Openers	___	___	___	___	___
Decoration	___	___	___	___	___
Triple "-ly" Adverbs	___	___	___	___	___

Conclusion	V.
Repeats three themes (topics)	___
Most important? Why?	___
Least important? Why?	___
Stylistic techniques (at your level)	___

Unit VIII: Essay Composition
Lesson 21: The Faith of St. Francis Completed

Objective
To study the fundamentals of essay writing by revising and expanding a previously written report. (Lessons 21 and 22 give assignments with the basic and extended essay forms, which should suffice for students of all levels, however if students require a more difficult and sophisticated level of essay writing, please proceed to the super-essay format found in the *Teaching Writing: Structure & Style* seminar and book.)

Source Text
Sources from Lesson 11: The Faith of St. Francis (page 59), as well as any other references or commentaries you choose.

Assignment
1. Find your completed 3-paragraph report on The Faith of St. Francis from Lesson 11. This will provide the body for your essay. Edit and rewrite these three paragraphs using your newer, more advanced stylistic techniques. You will see how much you have learned!
2. Consider what type of background information would fit nicely to form the introduction, as well as what might be seen as the most significant idea to focus on in the conclusion.

Structure & Style Tools and Suggestions
One significant difference between a "report" and an "essay", is that in an essay you must analyze the facts or details rather than just state them. The conclusion is the critical element of an essay, and should include your opinion or original ideas, although it is important to avoid using "I think…" or "In my opinion…" statements. Your conclusion must state what is the most important or significant topic or aspect of a topic.

Before writing, and as part of your preparation, search for other sources. If you have access to an encyclopedia, you might look up "St. Francis" and take some notes, remembering the specific topic of "Faith – how was it practiced by St. Francis?" Focus your search toward finding topics which could potentially answer the main question. Ultimately, in an essay, you must give your own opinion as to which theory or theme seems most convincing to you. Find support for your theory/theme in order to strengthen your essay.

Checksheet for Lesson 21

Levels A, B, & C

Presentation
___ title centered and underlined
___ name, date
___ clearly presented
___ space between paragraphs

Mechanics
___ indent paragraphs
___ complete sentences
___ capitals (uppercase)
___ punctuation

Structure
___ follows model
___ paragraphs roughly equal size
___ topic and clincher sentences
(BODY PARAGRAPHS ONLY)
___ repeat or reflect 2-3 key words
___ title reflects key words of final sentence in Conclusion **or** last sentence of Introduction

Style Tools
___ underline dress-ups (one of each)
___ no "banned" adjectives
___ no "banned" verbs

Sentence Openers
___ ❶ subject
___ ❷ preposition
___ ❸ "-ly" word
___ ❹ "ing"/"ed" opener
___ ❺ adverb clausal opener
___ ❻ VSS (<5 words)

Introduction	I.
setting/historical background	___
states three topics	___
poses a question	___
dress-up	___
sentence openers	___
decoration (B&C)	___
triple "-ly" adverbs (C)	___

Body Paragraphs	II.	III.	IV.
topic/clincher related	___	___	___
dress up	___	___	___
sentence openers	___	___	___
decoration (B&C)	___	___	___
triple "-ly" adverbs (B&C)	___	___	___
strong verb	___	___	___

Conclusion	V.
repeats three themes (topics)	___
most important? Why?	___
answers question	___
dress-up	___
sentence openers	___
decoration (B&C)	___
triple "-ly" adverbs (C)	___

Note: Please customize this checklist for each student by crossing off techniques not understood.

Lesson 22: What are the Responsibilities of a Christian?

Objective
To practice writing an extended (6 or 7 paragraph) essay.

Source Text
There are many readings from the Bible which address the question of what it means to be a responsible Christian. You may draw from any part of the Bible that would help you address this subject. Below is a list of passages to help you get started. Read these selections of Holy Scripture (and others as directed by your parent or teacher), taking brief notes of possible topics. For an extended essay, you will need 4 or 5 that seem most significant or interesting to you. Mother Teresa, St. Francis and Abraham Lincoln all read their Bibles daily and their prayer lives were built upon the foundation of Holy Scripture. Consider the key virtues of their respective characters. How do these virtues connect with the topics you will discern from reading your Bible? What made Mother Teresa, St. Francis and Abraham Lincoln responsible Christians?

Assignment
Write a 6 or 7 paragraph essay (your choice) on the responsibilities of a Christian. Apply all the essay writing ideas from previous lessons, but expand the body of your essay to include 4 or 5 topics. Follow the *Extended Essay Model* below. Be sure to stress in your conclusion what is the **most significant/important thing and why.**

SCRIPTURAL SOURCES	EXTENDED ESSAY MODEL
	I. Introduction
Romans 12	1. Attention
Romans 13	2. Background info (time, place)
Romans 15: 1-7	3. State the 4 or 5 themes (topics)
Galatians 5: 13-26	II. Topic A
Galatians 6: 1-10	Details
Ephesians 4: 17-32	Clincher
Ephesians 6: 1-18	III. Topic B
Colossians 3: 1-25	Details
Colossians 4: 1-6	Clincher
1 Thessalonians 5: 12-22	IV. Topic C
Hebrews 10: 19-25	Details
Hebrews 12: 1-14	Clincher
James (all chapters)	V. Topic D
1 Peter 1: 13-19	Details
1 Peter 2: 1-20	Clincher
1 Peter 3: 1-17	VI. Conclusion
1 Peter 5: 5-9	1. Restate the 4 or 5 topics
	2. Most significant & WHY

Review the Essay-Writing Process

1. Read the Scripture selections, noting possible themes (topics):

   _____   _____
   _____   _____
   _____   _____
   _____   _____

2. Choose the 4 or 5 most significant or interesting topics.
3. Plan your composition according to the model.
4. Take notes from the source texts, fusing ideas from different sources if they relate to the same topic.
5. Supplement your details with comments you may have about each topic.
6. Write your body paragraphs first, using all the stylistic techniques that you have learned.
7. After the body paragraphs are written, write your introduction and conclusion. Be careful to use a decoration to grab the reader's attention in the introduction, and make a strong statement as to what is most significant and why in your conclusion.

Advanced students may want to take this opportunity to write a significantly more in-depth analysis of the responsibilities of a Christian, and discuss more than five themes. In that case, one of the following "Super" essay models would provide a way to organize a multitude of topics. As is evident from the diagrams below, a Super essay consists of two (or three) Basic (or Extended) essays on related subjects glued together with a "super-introduction" and a "super-conclusion." In such a case, much more commentary and depth of analysis is required.

Advanced students should refer to their MLA Handbook for the proper structuring of a bibliography and handling of quotations and footnotes.

THE SUPER ESSAY MODEL	THE SUPER-DUPER ESSAY MODEL
I. SUPER - INTRODUCTION II. Introduction - Essay One III. Topic A IV. Topic B V. Topic C VI. Conclusion – Essay One VII. Introduction – Essay Two VIII. Topic D IX. Topic E X. Topic F XI. Topic G XII. Conclusion – Essay Two XIII. SUPER - CONCLUSION	I. SUPER - INTRODUCTION II. Introduction – Essay One III. Topic A IV. Topic B V. Topic C VI. Conclusion – Essay One VII. Introduction – Essay Two VIII. Topic D IX. Topic E X. Topic F XI. Topic G XII. Conclusion – Essay Two XIII. Introduction – Essay Three XIV. Topic H XV. Topic I XVI. Topic J XVII. Topic K XVIII. Conclusion – Essay Three XIX. SUPER - CONCLUSION

Checksheet for Lesson 22

Levels A, B, & C

Presentation
___ title centered and underlined
___ name, date
___ clearly presented
___ space between paragraphs

Mechanics
___ indent paragraphs
___ complete sentences
___ capitals (uppercase)
___ punctuation

Structure
___ follows model
___ paragraphs roughly equal size
___ topic and clincher sentences
(BODY PARAGRAPHS ONLY)
___ repeat or reflect 2-3 key words
___ title reflects key words of final sentence in Conclusion **or** last sentence of Introduction

Style Tools
___ underline dress-ups (one of each)
___ no "banned" adjectives
___ no "banned" verbs

Sentence Openers
___ ❶ subject
___ ❷ preposition
___ ❸ "-ly" word
___ ❹ "ing"/"ed" opener
___ ❺ adverb clausal opener
___ ❻ VSS (<5 words)

Introduction — I.
setting/historical background ___
states three topics ___
poses a question ___
end with title ___
dress-up ___
sentence openers ___
decoration (B&C) ___
triple "-ly" adverbs (C) ___

Body Paragraphs — II. III. IV. V. (VI.)

	II.	III.	IV.	V.	(VI.)
topic/clincher related	___	___	___	___	___
dress up	___	___	___	___	___
sentence openers	___	___	___	___	___
decoration	___	___	___	___	___
triple "-ly" adverbs	___	___	___	___	___
strong verb	___	___	___	___	___

Conclusion — VI. (VII.)
repeats three themes (topics) ___
most important? Why? ___
answers question ___
dress-up ___
sentence openers ___
decoration (B&C) ___
triple "-ly" adverbs (C) ___

Note: Please customize this checklist for each student by crossing off techniques not understood. This page may be photocopied for use with future essays.

Critique Vocabulary Thesaurus

The thesaurus below provides alternatives to words that you might overuse when you write critiques. The synonyms are arranged according to the paragraph where you might need them. As you will see in the next unit, you can use any of the synonyms below to replace less descriptive options. Not all of the words can be used interchangeably, so you must learn the terms and know when to use each one. The exercise which follows the thesaurus will help develop your knowledge of these terms.

Introduction

Story tale, saga, narrative, epic, legend, mystery, tragedy, comedy, romance, novel, yarn, anecdote, myth

Type sad, nature, science fiction, love, adventure, historical, horror, folk, fairy, animal, moral, space, descriptive

Characters

(players, actors, heroes, personae, participants, figures, villain, victim)

Role main, central, leading, major, minor, subordinate, lesser, supporting, shadowy, background, secondary

Type adventurous, tragic, comic, bumbling, retiring, extroverted, pliant, scheming, sordid, acquisitive, inquisitive, impulsive, sinister

Analysis well- or poorly-drawn, convincing, fully or underdeveloped, consistent, lifeless, too perfect, overly evil, idyllic

Setting

Time long ago, ancient, Medieval, modern, contemporary, futuristic, mythical

Place rural, urban, small town, frontier, pioneer, war, space, slums, ghetto, exotic, foreign land

Mood mysterious, foreboding, tragic, bland, comic, violent, suspenseful, compelling, sad, supernatural, emotional

Conflict/Plot
(plan, conspiracy, scheme, intrigue, subplot, sequence of events, action, narrative, episode)

Stages   initiated, promoted, continued, expanded, resolved

Intensity   exacerbated, heightened, lessened

Analysis   over- or under-played, realistic, unrealistic, convincing, contrived, stretched, sketchy

Climax   turning point, most exciting moment, dramatic event, high point, crisis, anticlimactic, inevitable, conclusion

Analysis

Theme   message, moral, lesson, topic, subtheme, matter, subject

Techniques   foreshadowing, symbolism, quality of language, short sentences, repetition, relation of subplot to the narrative

***

Thesaurus Assignment

1. Using the Critique Vocabulary Thesaurus and a dictionary if needed, fill in the most appropriate words for the following:

    a. A long involved story of heroic achievements such as the Icelandic prose narrative - _____

    b. A true or fictitious narrative - _____

    c. A written account of connected events in order of happening - _____

    d. A long story with heroic figures, large crowds and events, relative and whole nations - _____

    e. A traditional narrative usually involving supernatural or imaginary persons - _____

    f. A short account of an interesting or entertaining incident - _____

    g. An incredible, usually magical story - _____

h. A fiction based on technological advances, frequently portraying time travel or life on other planets - _____

i. A book where fictitious persons are blended into actual historical events - _____

2. Give four synonyms for each of the following, using words from the thesaurus.

   a. participants _____

   b. scheme of events _____

   c. subject matter _____

   d. foreboding _____

   e. emotional crisis _____

3. List three stages in the development of the conflict:
   _____

4. List three literary devices or techniques:
   _____

5. What literary technique is used to:

   a. hint at future events? _____

   b. give emphasis? _____

   c. use one thing to hint at another? _____

   d. startle the reader? _____

117

Unit IX: Reviews or Critiques
Lesson 23: Mother Teresa Revisited

Objective
To begin writing critiques which follow the 3-paragraph model demonstrated in Unit III but add an introduction and conclusion.

Source Text

"I was surprised in the West to see so many young boys and girls given into drugs, and I tried to find out why - why is it like that, and the answer was: because there is no one in the family to receive them. Father and mother are so busy they have no time. Young parents are in some institution and the child takes back to the street and gets involved in something. We are talking of peace. These are things that break peace, but I feel the greatest destroyer of peace today is abortion, because it is a direct war, a direct killing—direct murder by the mother herself. And we read in the Scripture, for God says very clearly: Even if a mother could forget her child—I will not forget you—I have carried you in the palm of my hand. We are carried in the palm of His hand, so close to Him that unborn child has been carried in the hand of God. And that is what strikes me most, the beginning of that sentence, that even if a mother could forget something—impossible—but even if she could forget—I will not forget you. And today the greatest means - the greatest destroyer of peace is abortion. And we who are standing here - our parents wanted us. We would not be here if our parents would do that to us. Our children, we want them, we love them, but what of the millions."

"Many people are very, very concerned with the children in India, with the children in Africa where quite a number die, maybe of malnutrition, of hunger and so on, but millions are dying deliberately by the will of the mother. And this is what is the greatest destroyer of peace today. Because if a mother can kill her own child - what is left for me to kill you and you to kill me - there is nothing between. And this I appeal in India, I appeal everywhere: Let us bring the child back, and this year being the child's year: What have we done for the child? At the beginning of the year I told, I spoke everywhere and I said: Let us make this the year that we make every single child born, and unborn, wanted. And today is the end of the year, have we really made the children wanted? I will give you something terrifying. We are fighting abortion by adoption, we have saved thousands of lives, we have sent words to all the clinics, to the hospitals, police stations - please don't destroy the child, we will take the child. So every hour of the day and night it is always somebody, we have quite a number of unwedded mothers - tell them come, we will take care of you, we will take the child from you, and we will get a home for the child. And we have a tremendous demand from families who have no children that is the blessing of God for us."

"And also, we are doing another thing that is very beautiful - we are teaching our beggars, our leprosy patients, our slum dwellers, and our people of the street,

> natural family planning. In Calcutta alone in six years - it is all in Calcutta - we have had 61,273 babies less from the families who would have had, but because they practice this natural way of abstaining, of self-control, out of love for each other. We teach them the temperature meter, which is very beautiful, very simple, and our poor people understand. And you know what they have told me? Our family is healthy, our family is united, and we can have a baby whenever we want. So clear - those people in the street, those beggars - and I think that if our people can do like that how much more you and all the others who can know the ways and means without destroying the life that God has created in us."

Assignment

1. Reread the source text excerpt from Mother Teresa's 1979 speech of acceptance for the Nobel Peace Prize. This is the same source text that you began to critique in Lesson 6. Note: The entire length of Mother Teresa's Nobel Lecture was seven pages (25 paragraphs). The above excerpt you are critiquing represents just three of the total number of paragraphs. Her lecture was delivered in Oslo, Norway on December 11, 1979. You can view the entire speech and/or listen to a sound recording of Mother Teresa's speech by visiting: http://nobelprize.org/nobel_prizes/peace/laureates/1979/teresa-lecture.html on the Internet.
2. Revisit the outline you created using the story sequence chart for the three body paragraphs in Lesson 6.
3. Use the tools below to outline the introduction and conclusion you will now be adding.
4. Finally, rewrite your own critique adding the new elements you have learned since Lesson 6 to the three body paragraphs. Also, add your new introduction and conclusion paragraphs.

Structural tools and Suggestions

Find and follow your story sequence model in Lesson 6. The objective of this present lesson is to take a story summary and expand it into a more objective review, or simple critique.

Introductions

In general, critique introductions must include certain necessary pieces of information. You may include additional information as well, but the following are the required elements:

1. Story, book, speech, video, or other title
2. Author, and short biographical information
3. Date of publication or first presentation
4. Number of pages, length of presentation
5. Pictures (if any) – number and quality

Conclusions

Critique conclusions should include your opinions about what was strong or weak in the story, book, speech, video or other presentation and why, what you liked best and least and why. The conclusion should generally include the following:

1. Likes and strengths. Why?
2. Dislikes and weaknesses. Why?
3. Overall meaning and value of the story, book, speech or video.
4. Words reflecting the title (at end of the paragraph).

The "why" commentary is crucial because it provides the reader with what you believe to be the most important point of the story, book, speech or video. Again, however, avoid using the word "I" and expressions such as "I think..." and "I believe..."

Checksheet for Critiques - Lessons 23 & 24

| **Presentation**
___ title centered and underlined
___ name, date
___ clearly presented
___ space between paragraphs
___ no banned words
___ underline dress-ups

Mechanics
___ indent paragraphs
___ complete sentences
___ punctuation

Structure
___ follows model
___ paragraphs roughly equal size
___ title reflects final sentence of first paragraph and/or last paragraph

Sentence Openers
___ ❶ subject
___ ❷ preposition
___ ❸ "-ly" word
___ ❹ "ing"/"ed" opener
___ ❺ adverb clausal opener
___ ❻ VSS (<5 words) | **Introduction**   I.

story/book/speech/video title ___
author's name ___
publication information ___
number of pages, etc. ___
dress-up ___
sentence openers ___
decoration ___
triple "-ly" adverbs ___

Body Paragraphs   II.   III.   IV.

dress up   ___ ___ ___
sentence openers   ___ ___ ___
decoration   ___ ___ ___
triple "-ly" adverbs   ___ ___ ___

Conclusion   V.

liked/strengths, why? ___
disliked/weaknesses, why? ___
value, significance, why? ___
dress-up ___
sentence openers ___
decoration ___
triple "-ly" adverbs ___

Note: Please customize this checklist for each student by crossing off techniques not understood. This page should be photocopied for use with future critiques. |

Lesson 24: The Gettysburg Address
Gettysburg, Pennsylvania
November 19, 1863

Objective
To practice critique writing.

Source Text

> Four score and seven years ago our fathers brought forth on this continent, a new nation, conceived in Liberty, and dedicated to the proposition that all men are created equal.
>
> Now we are engaged in a great civil war, testing whether that nation, or any nation so conceived and so dedicated, can long endure. We are met on a great battle-field of that war. We have come to dedicate a portion of that field, as a final resting place for those who here gave their lives that that nation might live. It is altogether fitting and proper that we should do this.
>
> But, in a larger sense, we can not dedicate—we can not consecrate—we can not hallow—this ground. The brave men, living and dead, who struggled here, have consecrated it, far above our poor power to add or detract. The world will little note, nor long remember what we say here, but it can never forget what they did here. It is for us the living, rather, to be dedicated here to the unfinished work which they who fought here have thus far so nobly advanced. It is rather for us to be here dedicated to the great task remaining before us—that from these honored dead we take increased devotion to that cause for which they gave the last full measure of devotion—that we here highly resolve that these dead shall not have died in vain—that this nation, under God, shall have a new birth of freedom—and that government of the people, by the people, for the people, shall not perish from the earth.

Assignment
Write a critique of the Gettysburg Address. For this assignment you will find it very helpful to use other books (or the Internet) to find extra information for your composition. The Gettysburg Address was very short, but oh so powerful. Follow the checksheet on page 121.

Style Tools and Examples
Practice using triple clauses in your compositions. For instance,

> What was President Lincoln doing? Three things – visualizing, dedicating, resolving

Now construct a sentence with triple clauses:

President Lincoln was successful and cherished because he knew how to visualize a nation under God, because he dedicated himself and others to that vision, and because he resolved that the dead shall not have died in vain.

Using the following phrases and words (or variants of them), create sentences with triple clauses.

1. Why did St. Francis leave home and the wealth of his father? (disobeyed, obeyed, humble)

   (who)_____
   _____

   (because)_____
   _____

2. Why did Mother Teresa cling to the poor of Calcutta? (respected, loved, loyal)

   (who)_____
   _____

   (because)_____
   _____

3. Why did Abraham want to marry Mary Todd? (simple, kind, motherly)

   (who)_____
   _____

   (because)_____
   _____

Congratulations!

You have finished the 24 character-based writing lessons in this book. Undoubtedly, you have improved your writing skills, but hopefully you have also learned to think a bit more about your own character development and the importance of prayer, Holy Scripture, key virtues and solid relationships in your life. It's never about me, it's never about you - it's always about us! The grace of God works most abundantly in the spaces between us. Our character does not develop in a vacuum – it develops in community – in relationship with others.

You also have completed lessons from all nine units of the *Teaching Writing: Structure & Style* syllabus, and should now be able to design your own writing projects using any source of information. Although you probably have your style checklist memorized by now, you might like to remove some of the checksheets, charts and lists from this book and keep them in a notebook for future reference.

I sincerely hope that you have begun a process of writing practice, reading, critical thinking, contemplation, and character development that will continue throughout your life. Remember, virtues are the essence of the human spirit and the content of our character. We become the virtues we practice. May the person you become be for the glory of God! May our gracious Lord bless you and all your efforts abundantly, that you may grow in faith, hope, and love! Peace in Christ Jesus.

About the Author

Daniel Weber currently serves as Chaplain at the Atascadero State Hospital, while teaching part-time at Cal Poly. Previously, he was C.E.O. of a semiconductor equipment company, and holds an M.B.A. from Pepperdine University as well as an M.P.S. (Pastoral Studies) from Loyola University. He has had published a wide range of academic articles and holds four U.S. patents.

He lives in Atascadero, California with his wife of 25 years, their two children and dog, Dixie. Throughout his career and life, Daniel has worked to improve his own character, committing himself to the ideal of servant leadership.